PRAISE FOR *OUTSMARTED*

"Lisa Green's *Outsmarted* is a deeply useful, practical guide for educators who struggle to teach in the presence of smartphones. I wish I'd had a copy of the book when I began teaching fifteen years ago, and many of Green's tips are even more useful today as phones continue to play a growing role in the classroom and in the lives of students across the globe."

—**Adam Alter,** *New York Times*' bestselling author of *Irresistible*

"Lisa Green has created a transformative guide for educators to navigate the digital age. It offers practical tools and forward-thinking strategies to engage iGen students deeply influenced by smartphones and social media. This book is a must-read for anyone looking to evolve their teaching methods and prepare students for a world shaped by technology."

—**Eric Sheninger,** speaker, author of *Digital Leadership*

"Undeniably, the single most powerful tool to impact our students' lives is the smartphone. Love it or hate it, we are teaching in an era of advanced technology, a learning landscape that can either result in complacent experiences in school for our students or empowering ones. Lisa Green hits the nail on the head with this exploration of how to teach meaningfully in a classroom full of devices. She examines how to create purpose, belonging, and intention with practical strategies that make my inquiry heart sing. Lisa's work is a welcomed addition to the field and a book sure to be on every teacher's must-read' list."

—**Trevor MacKenzie,** best-selling author of *Dive into Inquiry* and the *Inquiry Mindset* series

OUTSMARTED

THE CHANGING FACE OF LEARNING IN THE ERA OF SMARTPHONES AND TECHNOLOGY

LISA GREEN

© 2024 by Lisa Green

All rights reserved. No part of this publication may be reproduced in any form or by any electronic or mechanical means, including information storage and retrieval systems, without permission in writing by the publisher, except by a reviewer who may quote brief passages in a review. For information regarding permission, contact the publisher at elevatebooksedu.com.

> These books are available at special discounts when purchased in quantity for use as premiums, promotions, fundraising and educational use. For inquiries and details, contact the publisher at elevatebooksedu.com.

Published by Elevate Books EDU

Library of Congress Control Number: 2024950773
Paperback ISBN: 979-8-9913909-4-1
eBook ISBN: 979-8-9913909-5-8

This book is dedicated to my wife, Natalie.
Thank you for encouraging me up all the
summits in my life.

CONTENTS

How to Read This Book vii
Author's Note ix

Chapter 1: ~~A Problem~~ An Opportunity 1
Chapter 2: Understanding Today's Teen 11
Chapter 3: Phone Management 19
Chapter 4: Assessment in the Era of Smartphones and Technology 29
Chapter 5: Authentic Assessment Involves The Student 45
Chapter 6: Testing and Assessment in the Era of Smartphones and Technology 69
Chapter 7: Build the Skills 85
Chapter 8: Textbook to Tech and the Loss of Shared Experience 99
Chapter 9: Getting Back to Group Work 109
Chapter 10: Embracing The Tech 121
Chapter 11: The Digital Classroom 135
Chapter 12: Evaluating Student Work 153
Chapter 13: Put It into Practice 163
Chapter 14: My Final Thoughts on Open AI and Technology . . . 177

Glossary of Technology 183
Acknowledgments 187
About the Author 188
Citations 189
More From Elevate Books EDU 193

HOW TO READ THIS BOOK

My intention was to make this book interactive and to provide you with opportunities for introspection. *Outsmarted* contains practical ideas for educators, but it is meant for anyone, including parents, who is interested in how learning and understanding need to adapt to the educational landscape of the digital world. I encourage you to read this book with others. The act of discussing concepts and your ideas and experiences with others is a powerful learning tool in this advanced era of technology where AI is beginning to think for us.

Throughout the book, you will find Pause for Thought exercises that are intended to push and encourage you to think about, discuss, and understand modern learning challenges.

Happy reading!

AUTHOR'S NOTE

I was on a kayaking expedition when someone asked me, "What kind of teacher do you think you are?" The person who posed the question was a twenty-one-year-old traveller from the United Kingdom whom I had only just met.

In all my years of teaching, I had never been asked this question or given myself time to think about it. After taking a few minutes to reflect, I responded, "I think . . . I *hope* I am the kind of teacher who inspires my students to love learning. I want my students to leave my class genuinely excited to learn all they can about the world and themselves. That is the teacher I hope I am."

I believe we are here to learn as much as we can while we can. Although that was the first time I had put those thoughts into words, that philosophy is at the core of who I am as a teacher and a human being. It's what drove me to write this book. Thank you for picking it up and for your commitment to learning and teaching.

We are all teachers of some kind. "What kind of a teacher do you think you are?"

CHAPTER 1

~~A PROBLEM~~
AN OPPORTUNITY

We have a problem. Sorry to start with a doomsday-like statement, but if you work or live with young adults, you probably already know that smartphones are majorly impacting how today's ~~screenagers~~ teenagers function, socialize, and learn.

Walk into any educational staff room, and you are likely to hear voices of complaint and frustration about the issues smartphones bring to the classroom—from distractions to cheating to simply letting technology do the work of thinking. More than anyone else, teachers and educational staff are witnessing the repercussions of a generation that has grown up in the era of the internet, smartphones, and social media. Today's students do not know a world without it.

In her article "Have Smartphones Destroyed a Generation," psychologist Jean M. Twenge fittingly dubbed the group born between 1995 and 2012, the iGen. While most generations are defined or shaped by events—the Great Depression, wars, and 9/11—smartphones and social media have impacted the iGen at an exponential rate never seen before, and the consequences of which society has yet to understand. While events that define a generation usually impact different areas of society, in different parts of the world, with different economic backgrounds in different ways, researchers note that "the twin rise of the smartphone and social media has caused an earthquake of a magnitude not seen in a very long time, if ever," and it is being felt everywhere across the globe. Positive or negative, society is starting to see the effects.

Parents may be breathing a sigh of relief as many of today's teens are physically safer than perhaps they were at the same age. They don't worry quite as much about their teens leaving the house, driving, drinking, and having sex because the kids are more likely to be home or findable with the tap of an app. While some risks have decreased, others have risen. Before the pandemic, mental health was at an all-time low for tweens and teens, with skyrocketing rates of depression and suicide. The lockdowns of 2020 resulted in more screen and phone time, not less.

Many teens today prefer to spend time with their peers online. The fact that they are staying at home more means that they are physically experiencing the world less as well as working and socializing less. And it is not just teens. Since the pandemic lockdowns, there has been a growing trend of staying at home for all ages. Bloomberg is calling this the "Introvert Economy," with more people spending their money ordering in and doing in-home activities.

The result of less socializing is that the iGen is more immature than previous generations, with eighteen-year-olds acting more like fifteen-year-olds, and fifteen-year-olds acting more like thirteen-year-olds. Teachers, including myself, are noticing the effects of this rise in immaturity, such as a general lack of social skills compared to students of previous years. For the first ten years of my teaching career, I believed that kids were growing up too fast. I suppose an argument could be made that a maturity slowdown is not necessarily negative, but the lack of social skills and the rising number of students who prefer to be on their phones rather than speak to one another is concerning. In the article, "An 8-Week Group Cognitive Behavioral Therapy Intervention for Mobile Dependence," researchers who studied Chinese college students' dependency on smartphones suggest it could very well be that "in the next decade, we may see more adults who know just the right emoji for a situation, but not the right facial expression." Unfortunately, the impacts do not stop there.

Pew Research released in 2019 found that 96 percent of teenagers had access to a smartphone, and 45 percent admitted to feeling addicted to their smartphone. While 60 percent said they would rather spend time with friends online than in real life, 52 percent said they wanted to cut back on their smartphone usage. Teenagers themselves are starting to recognize the negative side effects of too much time spent on their phones. What are we doing to help them?

> **45 PERCENT OF TEENS ADMITTED TO FEELING ADDICTED TO THEIR SMARTPHONE.**
>
> —*Pew Research*

Social media companies have admitted to creating addictive platforms that are meant to engage and monopolize the time of their users. Corporations used to want consumers' money, but now they want our time and attention. The more the better. Receiving a *like*, a *heart*, or seeing the number of people who have watched a *snap* rise releases dopamine in the brain, triggering feelings of satisfaction and pleasure. Repeated dopamine hits are how addictions form. It feels good, so we click again and again. What is a struggle for adults is even more so for teens whose lack of self-control leaves them particularly susceptible to social media's draw. Today's smartphone is like the enchanted spindle, the poisoned apple, and the house made of candy in the middle of the woods; our teenagers can't help themselves from falling under its spell and becoming increasingly dependent on it.

The study that examined mobile phone dependence in Chinese college students listed the following as some of the symptomatic behaviours of smartphone dependency:

- Excessive and unreasonable use in public places
- Impulse control
- Used to regulate emotions
- Negative consequences in daily life
- Rationalization of use
- Symptoms of withdrawal without access

I certainly have seen many of these symptoms with the majority of young adults I teach, and my guess is that you have too.

Call it the "Introvert Economy" or the "Attention Economy;" all signs point to the fact that smartphones, social media, and technology have us interacting with screens more and with one another less. In a culture where remote work and shopping from home are increasingly common, schools have become one of the few physical spaces for social interaction and relationship-building. So for all the challenges facing educators today, we have a unique opportunity, and perhaps responsibility, to teach students essential interpersonal skills and real-life communication skills.

PAUSE FOR THOUGHT

- Given the technological changes in the world today, is it time to reconsider the purpose of school? What could this look like?
- How can the physical school environment play a unique role in promoting social interaction and interpersonal skills development?

FIGHT, FLIGHT, OR ADAPT

Smartphones have fully infiltrated middle and high school classrooms. From my personal experience, I average maybe one or two students per class who do not have a smartphone on them. These anomalies may exist because a student has broken their phone or, on a very rare occasion, had it taken away as punishment by a parent. It is far more common to see a student without a smartphone because they have low or no battery left from using it so much throughout the day. Teachers face an ongoing battle for attention, and it often feels like we're losing. It's not as if we're not trying, but students' habits are hard to break.

During the **first few weeks** of class, students stream into the room, find their seats, and pull out their phones. I ask them to put their phones away and remove their earbuds. And then I wait a minute or two for them to actually do it. Once they've disconnected, I ask them to make sure their phones are out of sight so they do not feel tempted during class. Oh, and I clarify that I meant *both* earbuds and yes, I can still see them in their ears, even underneath the hoods.

Looking around the room, I can see that for many students, somewhere "out of sight" means on their desk in front of them, so I clarify that "out of sight" means in your bag. I wait again, and this time notice how every available outlet has been hijacked by a snake-like white power cord venomously sucking life back into the dying and dead.* With class finally beginning, I turn my back for a second to write on the board, move a presentation slide, or grab a sheet, only to find that when I turn back, lo and behold, a handful of students are staring at their screens. I ask again for students to put their phones away, wait, wait some more, and then try to begin again.

This mini battle of wills repeats multiple times throughout the class. My emotions fluctuate from feelings of anger and frustration at being ignored by students to disappointment and confusion as to why students simply do not want to learn. I can't help but worry that my colleagues will think less of me when they peer into my room and see so many students disengaged from learning and on their phones. Any confidence in my teaching ability that I started the day with takes a kick to the gut as clearly whatever game, app, or text conversation they are looking at seems far more interesting than the grammar, vocabulary, or cultural lesson I have spent hours planning. And the truth is, it probably is! Frustrated, I wonder how I or any teacher compete with Snapchat streaks, Instagram feeds, the newest addictive game, or the latest gossip they're texting about with their friend in another class.

(*I have noticed an increase in some crafty students who, tired of scavenging for available outlets, have begun bringing power banks to school with them. I have also contemplated a side hustle of selling forgotten power cords on the tech black market.)

By **about a month** into the course, things don't appear to have changed all that much. The bell rings, and students stream into class, find their seats, and get on their phones. If I remember, I ask the students to put their phones away and unplug their earbuds, wait a minute or two for them to actually do it, then ask again that they put their phone somewhere out of sight so they do not feel tempted during class.

By **about two months** into the course, I've grown weary of the same old scene. Students stream into class, find their seats, and get on their phones. I smile, remind myself to breathe, and muster up the energy to remind the students to put their phones away. I try very hard not to snap at those who *forget*.

At **about three months,** students stream into the classroom, find their seats, and get on their phones. Defeated, I look at the calendar and remind myself there is a little over a month left, and I can start fresh with new classes. *I will be tougher with them, I will not give in so easily, and I can and will win this battle,* I think. Then I start the lesson, trying not to fantasize about other professions and wondering how early is too early for retirement.

Although school-wide phone bans have recently come into effect in many countries around the world, their impact will be largely dependent on individual teachers, and their overall success is yet to be determined. While banning phones may help with classroom management, it does not necessarily address the social, emotional, and overall cognitive impacts that educators note are on the rise as a result of excessive phone use.

A PROBLEMATIC WORLD FULL OF POTENTIAL

Smartphones, with their flashy screens, access to the internet, social media, and apps made their first appearance around the start of the 2000s, with Steve Jobs announcing the launch of the first iPhone in 2007. Students in high school today have grown up as the first smartphone generation, the repercussions of which, I believe, teachers are starting to recognize: smartphone addictive tendencies, a lack of social awareness and connection, a general disengagement from the world around them, to name just a worrying few.

Occasionally, I wonder if I am doing what every older generation does when looking at the younger. My parents and grandparents were worried that pop and rap music would "rot my brain," video games would make me stupid, and too much TV would ruin my eyes. I feel I turned out okay. However, I can't know because I will never know the me who could have grown up without all that, just as today's students have no idea who they could or would be without a smartphone in their hands.

SMART NUMBERS?

According to a recent study, teenagers spend on average eight hours a day staring at their smartphone screens.

Let's put that number into perspective with some simple math.

8 HOURS A DAY FOR 365 DAYS A YEAR = 2,920 HOURS A YEAR

If we assume that the average person sleeps for eight hours, that means **the average teenager spends half their waking hours looking at their smartphone.** Put another way, that's the equivalent of 182.5 days of the year staring at the smartphone screen.

OVER THE COURSE OF FIVE YEARS, THE AVERAGE TEENAGER WILL SPEND 912 DAYS, OR TWO-AND-A-HALF YEARS, STARING AT THEIR SMARTPHONE SCREEN.

Smartphones provide many functions in today's classroom: calculator, dictionary, encyclopedia, translator, and access to the internet where all the class information is held. Gamified learning apps, AI, and chatbots also provide many functions in today's learning and working world. Smartphones have the undeniable potential to be useful, but it is naïve to think that students have the willpower to limit themselves to the learning resources on their phones during class or even understanding that AI tools should be used to enhance their learning, not do the work for them. Until I have a time machine that can transport my entire class back to the 1990s or a remote that controls all the smartphone devices in my class, there are just too few of me to monitor what every student is doing on his or her phone or computer.

Smartphones and the apps that constantly vie for our attention are a part of our society. As educators, we can choose to battle against the machine and try desperately to convince our students that their phones and devices can never compare to the real-live-in-person-learning experience. We can put on a show for each class to vie for their attention, or we can buy phone caddies and become the in-class phone police. Alternatively, we can take a passive approach, throw up our hands, and try to ignore what we see, or perhaps find new professions.

Or we can accept that smartphones and technology are here to stay and try to adapt.

This book is for those who are open to adapting and those who believe that we must do a better job at helping the younger generations navigate and understand the digital world we all live in today. Their future—and ours—depends on it.

PAUSE FOR THOUGHT

Not to get too Orwellian, but there is nothing and nobody that knows more about you than your phone. Over the past few days, it has tracked where you have been, whom you have been with, how long you spent doing certain activities, your eating habits, your spending habits, what you are hoping to buy, where you are hoping to go, with whom you have talked and or texted, the kind of relationship you have with the people in your life based on how much you text and the tone that you use, what time you go to bed, what time you get up, and what you value. I could go on, but I think you're getting the point. Our phones have been programmed to know us better than we know ourselves. Our use of them goes far beyond simple communication; in fact, calling them *phones* seems like a misnomer when so few use them to talk to anyone.

Smartphone: Pleasure or Purpose?

1. If your phone could speak, what would it say about you?
2. What would it say about how you spend your time?
3. What would it say about what you value?
4. What would it say about your relationships?
5. In what ways do you use your phone as a purposeful tool?
6. In what ways do you use your phone for pleasure?

This is a fun get-to-know-you activity. It is also a great way to get students to start thinking about their relationship with their technology and just how much they use and rely on their phones.

CHAPTER 2

UNDERSTANDING TODAY'S TEEN

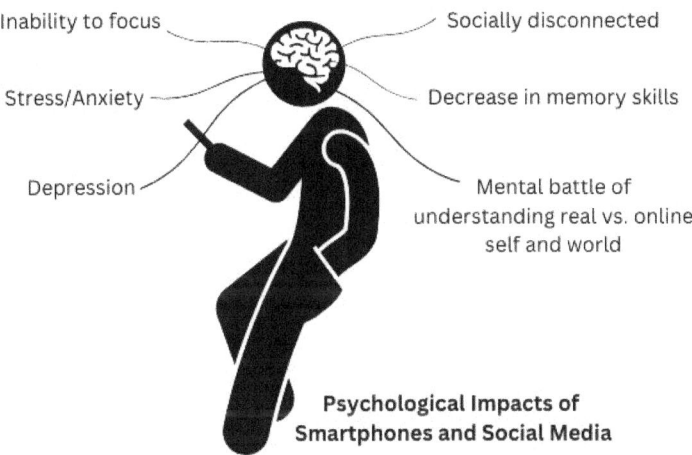

Psychological Impacts of Smartphones and Social Media

To understand the changing face of learning in the era of smartphones and technology, we must understand who today's youth are, what is impacting them, and how their generation is vastly different from the generations that came before them.

Today's teenagers have not grown up in and do not live in the same world as those of us who were born before the advent of handheld technology. For as long as they can remember, information and entertainment have been instantly available and calling for their attention. That's what the Attention Economy is all about: how much attention companies can capture from their targets. Advertisers used to focus on getting people to spend money. Today, their goal is to have us spend our time on things like apps, social media, YouTube, and streaming services, all of which are built with the explicit purpose of keeping their users online and on them. Employing the best psychological tactics, they work to ensure consumers' unsuspecting brains yield willingly to our devices.

We only have so much attention available to give to any one thing at any one time. Added to that reality is the fact that our capacity to focus our attention is limited. The result of this Attention Economy is that most humans seemingly do not possess the same amount of attention as they used to.

In his 2023 book, *Stolen Focus: Why You Can't Pay Attention and How to Think Deeply Again*, author Johann Hari dives into the causes and impacts of why so many of us are struggling to focus. Hari's book explores a myriad of factors that could be influencing focus and attention, including how advancing technology, screen use, and intentionally addictive algorithms have led to a dramatic increase in the amount of information we interact with and process, contributing to more stress, less sleep, and "stolen focus." Of particular note to me as an English teacher who has witnessed the challenge many students experience when faced with long form text, such as novel and multi-page articles, Hari explores how screens have impacted sustained reading practices by training the brain to read in a different way, scanning, skimming, and scrolling for information amidst blinking advertisements and buzzing text messages.

You may be feeling the effects of this yourself. Do you notice yourself zoning out while listening to a loved one or simply losing focus while reading this book? If you were a teen or young adult before the advent of smartphones, chances are good that you grew up reading books, watching full-length movies, waiting a week for your favourite sitcom to air, putting together LEGO projects, playing marathon-length board games like *Monopoly* and *Risk*, and generally figuring out how to entertain yourself. You've had years of practice focusing your attention, and yet you have probably noticed that it's difficult to focus these days.

Many of today's teens have never had the kind of practice focusing for long periods of time, so it's no surprise that they seem incapable of staying tuned in for very long into anything.

Telling someone to pay attention will not work when there is nothing left to pay it with. But all may not be lost! If the brain can become wired for distraction, there is hope that it can be rewired for deep focus.

> **IF THE BRAIN CAN BECOME WIRED FOR DISTRACTION, THERE IS HOPE THAT IT CAN BE REWIRED FOR DEEP FOCUS.**

NAVIGATING TWO SELVES

With online social media apps, today's teenagers are the most socially connected and yet socially disconnected generation of all time. They exist and manage their time in two worlds: the physical and the virtual. The separation between the two may seem normal to them, but the way it is impacting them is not. Many documentaries, articles, and movies focus on the effects of social media on mental health and depression. One of the most damaging effects is the result of living in a world where we have to represent, at a minimum, two selves: the real in-person self and the online self.

I am 100 percent guilty of representing my online self differently from who I am in real life. That's not to say that what or who I am putting out into the world is inauthentic. That is me climbing mountains,

river rafting, and genuinely enjoying life. Those images, however, reflect only a small portion of who I am and what my life is like. The more I represent myself one way, the more I feel pressure to continue representing myself that way. Pressure from where and from whom I can't say, but I feel pressure, nonetheless. Managing my online self, liking other people's posts, commenting, and sending messages to stay in touch with friends and family takes time and energy. As someone born in 1980, I never experienced this kind of pressure or other self to manage as a teenager, and I am thankful for that because it can be exhausting.

As an adult now, I understand that the online version of people's selves is not a representation of their whole selves. But, geez! It looks like everyone is having a good time all the time! For a young person, the false perceptions we have about what others' lives are like can be confusing. The delusions they may assume to be real can cause them to believe that they need to be representing themselves living their best life all the time. The act of mentally balancing, compartmentalizing, and deciphering true reality from the enhanced version of reality we see online takes a toll, one that I am not sure we fully understand yet.

BARRIERS TO COMMUNICATION AND CONNECTION

What we do understand (or at least recognize) is that teens today would rather communicate with one another via Snapchat, DMs, and text messages. I have witnessed two friends in the same room communicating on their phones instead of talking to one another. Is it that their online versions get along better than their in-person versions? Or is it that they feel they have nothing to talk about? Communication is a learned skill, and it involves more than just words. Communication is nuanced with verbal pauses, facial expressions, and tones of voice that, when understood, enhance a person's emotional quotient and empathy for the other. Even with emojis, these are subtleties that smartphones are not yet able to communicate.

In a technologically advanced world, with unlimited options of what to watch, read, and listen to, we are all watching, reading, and listening to different things. While I see many positives from the diversity of options allowing people to find anything that they are interested in, I am also worried that we are losing the socially shared experiences that allowed generations of the past to have something to talk about and connect over. Some of us get excited that the next season of our favourite streaming show is about to drop, but the idea of all of our friends watching the same thing at eight on a Monday night is almost unheard of now, as is the watercooler conversation the next morning. Even with my close friends, I often feel as if we are searching for something to connect on, and when we find that thing, the show we're watching or the book series we're reading, having a shared experience feels amazing. I will get into the ideas of how schools can still provide opportunities for shared experiences in later chapters, but for now, it is worth thinking about how the lack of shared experiences impacts not just the younger generation but society as a whole.

As human beings, we are built to socialize. It is why our species advanced over others. We learn by communicating, watching, and mimicking one another. Maybe we can still do all of those things socializing in an online environment, but I am skeptical. I've noticed that my current students do not behave in the socially responsible ways that my students from even a few years ago did. Overall, I see a general lack of empathy, a misunderstanding of social cues, and heightened anxiety about working with others. Certainly, I am not describing all my students, but it's an accurate depiction of far more than I would like for it to be.

DIGITAL AMNESIA

More concerning, at least to me, is the detrimental impact smartphones have on memory skills. Most of my students readily admit that they don't have a good memory or are bad at studying because they just can't remember the material. They aren't alone.

None of us needs to remember as much as we used to. I no longer need to remember phone numbers, birthdays, addresses, directions, meeting times, grocery items, passwords, or anything that my phone can keep track of for me. *Digital amnesia* is a term that is associated with those moments when we just can't seem to recall something we feel we should, or we forget an important event that we thought we had written down (like a friend's fiftieth birthday party . . . oops!). These forgetful moments, while forgivable and easily forgotten, may lead to something far more concerning.

My mom has dementia. She was diagnosed with it at fifty-eight years old. Over the past nine years, I have watched her slowly slip away. While the effects of the disease have been emotionally taxing, her experience has also made me hyper-aware and concerned about the D-word. This is personal for me. So when I read articles in which established neurobiologists express worries about the likelihood of a rise in dementia because of the reliance on smartphones, like the one from *The Guardian* titled, "Is your smartphone ruining your memory? A special report on the rise of 'digital amnesia,'" I get concerned.

While some neurobiologists note the benefits of smartphones freeing up our minds to do important work, others argue that smartphones cause us to pay less attention to what is going on around us, making it harder for us to "encode information in our memory," leading to fewer memories of events. While more research is needed, early evidence suggests that the very real threat smartphones pose by impacting our memory could potentially be causing "cortical thinning" in younger brains. Cortical thinning is normal, but as Larry Rosen, a psychologist who studies the effects of social media, technology, and the brain, points out, it's "supposed to happen at an older age." The concern is that this effect, which is associated with degenerative brain diseases, may lead to a future rise in earlier onset Alzheimer's and dementia.

Our grandparents and great-grandparents did not understand the dangers of smoking. When people began to put the pieces together, big tobacco companies glossed over their products' harmful effects. Still, I look at my family members who smoked and are suffering from the effects, and wonder, *How could you not have known or not thought it was bad for you?* I worry the same will be said to us by future generations when they reflect on our overuse of smartphones.

Some of my students roll their eyes when I express concern about their use and reliance on smartphones and technology. There are times when I feel like the crazy-conspiracy-theory lady who is running around the village trying to sound the alarm while everyone just laughs and aims their phones at me to document the moment and then turn it into a viral meme on social media. But as an adult and an educator who cares about the generations below me, I can't stop trying to sound that alarm. The future consequences are far too great.

PAUSE FOR THOUGHT

1. Do you think enough importance is being placed on the psychological impacts that smartphones are having on today's youth? At home? In society?

2. Do you think there needs to be more education about the psychological impacts of smartphones and technology in schools today? How could this be done?

3. When thinking about today's youth, what psychological impacts of smartphones and social media have you not considered before?
4. In your experience, what other ways do you think smartphones are psychologically impacting today's youth?

CHAPTER 3

PHONE MANAGEMENT

A*tomic Habits* author James Clear believes that five cues trigger good and bad habits:

1. Time
2. Location
3. Preceding event
4. Emotional state
5. Other people

When it comes to smartphone use, we may not be able to control these cues, but we can try to influence the impacts of some of them.

Clear believes that "location (i.e. environment) is the most powerful driver of mindless habits and also the least recognized," and that "our environment can either promote good habits or lead us toward bad ones."

The brain assigns specific cues to certain areas. Unfortunately, for most of my students, coming into class and sitting down at their desks triggers them to take out their phones and look at their screens. The reason this habit is so difficult to break, despite my consistent efforts, is that the cue triggers the same response in other classrooms, waiting rooms, bus stops, movie theatres, airports, sporting events, meetings, etc. Sitting down and waiting for something to begin has become a cue for most of society to take out their phones.

I am guilty of this myself. Are you? If you said yes, good for you. A well-known step to breaking a bad habit is admitting its existence. My own awareness of this habit means that now, when I am waiting for something to begin and I absentmindedly reach for my phone, I pause to reflect on why I am doing it. Is it: A) Because I am bored and just trying to kill time? B) Because the people around me are all looking at their phones? Or C) Because there is something I *really* need to look up or do on my phone? It is almost always a result of one of the first two.

> "WE FIRST MAKE OUR HABITS, THEN OUR HABITS MAKE US."
> —John Dryden

Getting teens to pause and reflect on *why* they are taking out their phones *when* they are taking out their phones may help to break the habit.

SMARTPHONE CHALLENGE: WHAT IS THE PURPOSE?

Every time you take out your phone for the next day, try to pause and ask yourself, *Why am I taking out my phone?* Answer this question before you do anything with your phone.

Bonus: Create a lock screen image with the text: Why am I taking out my phone?

Parents can do this with their children, and teachers can do this in class with their students.

Many students may answer that they want to play a certain game, access their music, or check their Snapchat, TikTok, Instagram, (Insert latest social media app here). While this may not be a valid answer to us, it is to them. Breaking the habit will be difficult because many teens do not recognize going on their phones as a bad habit. Further questions may need to be asked.

1. Why am I taking out my phone?
2. Why do I need to check my (insert social media app)?
3. Am I going on my phone because I am bored?
4. Am I going on my phone because everyone else is on theirs?
5. Do I *really* need to go on my phone *right* now?

SETTING THE SCENE

It is not uncommon to walk into a middle or high school classroom and see a cell phone pocket holder, or caddy, hanging from a wall. I believe these should be mandatory everywhere, from classrooms to restaurants. Every home should have a cell phone caddy hanging on the wall where family members and visiting friends can safely store their devices. While they may not be used all the time by everyone, a cell phone caddy is a physical signal and visual cue that the phones should take a back seat to the present company or activity at hand.

The physical space of your classroom is full of hidden cues. From garbage and recycling bins to hand-in boxes, these physical objects indicate appropriate behaviours from those in the space. Social programming has taught us that garbage should go in the garbage and paper should go in the paper recycling. When it comes to smartphone use, outside social behaviours do not promote responsible use of technology in the classroom, which means a few extra cues may be necessary.

CLASSROOM CUES TO PROMOTE A SOCIALLY RESPONSIBLE CLASSROOM ENVIRONMENT

- Smartphone caddy/holder hanging on a visually accessible wall or from individual desks
- Posters that indicate this is a learning environment
- A start-of-class reminder—"Okay everyone, we are about to start today's lesson and begin learning. Please finish whatever it is you are doing on your phones, log off, and put them in the cell phone caddy or in your bags."
- A slide at the beginning of a presentation with information about smartphone use, word of the day, cartoon, or puzzle that also includes a reminder—"Please put your phone out of sight before we begin to learn together."
- A note at the beginning of assignments that reminds students to rely on what they know and not on their phones, or a reminder that if they need to access a dictionary or translator on their phone, to use it appropriately.
- Modelling—Be aware of your own phone use and the example you set.

CREATING A PHONE AND TECHNOLOGY CONTRACT

It is important to let students know your phone and technology rules at the start of your class, but it is also important to have students create their own rules, guidelines, and consequences in a personal contract. Creating a personal contract lets students think about the ways in which the smartphone and technology impact their learning and the learning of others, and more importantly, it holds them accountable.

A teacher could come up with a class contract with the input of their students, have all students sign it, and then place that contract in a visible space within the classroom. Alternatively, students could create their own contracts that are kept in an easily accessible place. A contract makes the rules clear and the consequences equal for all. If it is a whole-class contract, everyone is involved, which means everyone should equally understand the rules. It's handy to have a contract to reference when a student takes their phone out or uses a little too much tech to help them with their work, or when a parent needs some clarity about the phone and tech rules in the class.

I have personally found that showing students an example or providing them with sentence starters can help facilitate the process. And yes, I recommend having students do this even in schools where smartphones are banned. Learners need to be aware of their habits in school and out. Making a plan to manage their technology use is a good habit to get into.

PHONE AND TECH USE (CONTRACT EXAMPLE)

I, _____, solemnly pledge to use my phone responsibly during class hours to ensure a focused and productive learning environment. In accordance with this commitment, I hereby agree to the following terms and conditions:

1. I will put my phone away at the beginning of every class before the teacher needs to ask me to.

2. I will keep my phone on silent mode or vibrate to minimise disruptions.
3. I will only use my phone for educational purposes, such as accessing class materials or conducting relevant research—and I will ask permission to do this.
4. I will refrain from texting, gaming, or engaging in any non-educational activities on my phone during class.
5. I will not use earbuds or headphones during lectures, discussions, or other class activities, unless specifically allowed by the instructor for a designated task.
6. I will not use AI chatbots or other automated services to complete academic work, including assignments, quizzes, or exams, unless expressly permitted by the instructor.
7. I will not rely on technology to substitute for my own understanding and effort in completing class assignments or participating in discussions.
8. I will not use my phone or other devices in a manner that may distract or disturb fellow students during class.
9. In case of emergencies, I will discreetly step out of the class to handle the situation and inform my instructor if necessary.
10. I understand that any violation of these terms may result in consequences, including but not limited to a warning, temporary confiscation of the device, or other measures determined by the instructor.
11. I acknowledge that exceptions may be granted for specific class activities or projects, with prior approval from the instructor.

By signing below, I affirm my commitment to responsible phone use and acknowledge the importance of maintaining a conducive learning environment for myself and my peers.

Student's Signature: _____ Date: _____

PHONE AND TECH USE (STUDENT EXAMPLE)

I, _____, in grade 10, solemnly swear to handle my phone and tech game with the utmost responsibility during class hours. Here is what I will try to commit to:

1. If I need to use a translator app, I'll ask the teacher first, no sly moves.
2. Chatbots and fancy tech tools are cool, but I won't use them to breeze through my assignments unless the teacher gives me the green light.
3. No disrupting the class vibes with my phone making noise or buzzing like crazy. Gotta keep it professional for everyone.
4. No headphone parties during class unless the teacher says it's game on for a specific task.
5. If there's an emergency, I'll ninja out of the class quietly and give the teacher a heads-up if needed.
6. I get it; breaking these rules might lead to consequences, like temporary tech confiscation or whatever consequences the teacher dishes out.

By signing below, I confirm that I will do my very best to follow these rules that I have set out for myself.

Student's Signature: _____ Date: _____

Remember to **be patient** when it comes to smartphone use in the classroom. You are not only promoting positive habits for your classroom, but you are also helping to promote socially responsible habits for everyday life. We all need reminders. This is why movie theatres and live productions all begin with an announcement reminding everyone to turn off or silence their devices. It is a social cue, and as we watch everyone around us follow that cue, we usually follow what others do around us.

PAUSE FOR THOUGHT

1. In what ways can you set the scene for responsible smartphone use in your own home or workplace?
2. For parents, in what ways do you educate your children about socially responsible phone use? Have you ever tried a phone-use contract with your children?

SETTING THE STANDARD AND FOLLOWING THROUGH

I don't know many teachers or parents who enjoy being the "bad guy." It doesn't feel good. I would far rather smile and laugh with my students than have to be strict and use my teacher voice. As teachers, however, our job is to help raise the adults of tomorrow. Many times that means having to remind students what proper societal behaviour looks like. When it comes to classroom expectations, it is far easier to start strict and become lenient than it is to start lenient and become strict.

In the first few weeks of a new class, it is imperative to set the tone and kind of environment that you want to see throughout the course. When it comes to smartphone use, this can mean constant reminders, taking phones away, and frustration on both sides. Stick with it and remind yourself (and your students) that you are not the phone police; you are guiding them to develop better habits that will help them to become more capable and confident adults.

Time and time again, I am reminded of just how much our students need us to be strict. Often, after having to reprimand a student for a specific undesirable behaviour and thinking that the student must say the nastiest things about me when they walk out the door, surprisingly, I find that same student requesting to be in my class again. I can't say this for all my experiences or speak for my students, but at the heart of it, I believe most children and teenagers just want our attention, to know they are seen, and to know that someone cares. I am sure that statement is surprising to no one, but I repeat it often, especially when having to be the "bad guy," because I need to remind myself of it.

PAUSE FOR THOUGHT

1. How do smartphones impact your classroom environment? (This may turn into a vent session, and that's okay because we all need a good vent, but when talking about what frustrates you, try to come up with ways to combat those negative behaviours).

2. In what ways can administrators and teachers support each other to help create a positive smartphone environment in the school?

3. How do you, or how can you, work with your students to promote positive social smartphone behaviour?

CHAPTER 4

ASSESSMENT IN THE ERA OF SMARTPHONES AND TECHNOLOGY

In March 2020, as a result of the COVID pandemic, schools around the world, including my own in British Columbia, quickly shifted from in-person to online learning models. While teachers scrambled to adjust the delivery of their lesson plans, larger questions about assessment were raised in staff meetings:

- *Should assessment practices be adjusted?*
- *How much should assignments be weighted?*
- *Given the situation, should students be penalised for not getting their work done?*

Granted, it was an unprecedented time. Questions around equity and fairness led to lengthy discussions about access to technology, outside resources, and support levels in the home. Concerns over students' social-emotional wellness flew to the forefront, as did considerations of the potential impact of stress on families brought on by the circumstances created by the pandemic. For a heartbeat, it felt like many in the academic world and beyond understood how inequitable and complex common assessment practices are. No one seemed to have an answer, and while everyone recognized the problem, no two districts, schools, or teachers approached the issue in the same way.

When the lockdowns lifted and schools returned to in-person learning, questions regarding the equity of assessment practices all but disappeared. The family stresses, economic inequalities, and life struggles that impact the social-emotional well-being of students never went away, and they never will. Those challenges, although highlighted by the pandemic, existed long before COVID-19. This is reality. In the next few chapters, we're going to bring some of these very real challenges into the spotlight once again. We'll look at how technology impacts the classroom experiences, student engagement and learning, and assessment practices. As we consider the world today's teenagers are living in, we'll also look at strategies to ensure that they understand how, when, why, and why not to rely on technology so that they learn to think for themselves.

QUICK HISTORY OF ASSESSMENT

In 1785, Yale instituted a grading system that ranked students using a four-point scale to create distinction categories for graduating students. Before this, oral exit exams were used in most institutions of higher learning to assess knowledge. Yale's original four-point scale is what many modern-day academic institutions model their GPA scale on. Nearly one hundred years later, in 1877, Harvard began using a 100-point scale and in 1883, quickly instituted the use of letter grades. But it was not until 1897, when Mount Holyoke implemented a grading system that combined percentages, letter grades, and written descriptions that the standardized grading practices many are familiar with today were adopted by other academic institutions at all levels in both the United States and Canada. While much has changed during the past one hundred twenty-five years, it seems that current grading practices have failed to advance. Life today, and certainly education, is nothing like it was in the 1800s, so why are many of our grading practices stuck in the past?

> A "GRADE CAN BE REGARDED ONLY AS AN INADEQUATE REPORT ON AN INACCURATE JUDGMENT BY A BIASED AND VARIABLE JUDGE OF THE EXTENT TO WHICH A STUDENT HAS ATTAINED AN UNDEFINED LEVEL OF MASTERY OF AN UNKNOWN PROPORTION OF AN INDEFINITE AMOUNT OF MATERIAL."
>
> —Paul Dressel, educational psychologist

WHAT AUTHENTIC ASSESSMENT LOOKS LIKE TODAY

Using the mountain as a learning journey metaphor, every class and all students start at the bottom at the beginning of the course and end at the top. The journey each individual student takes will be different. Some students may know the terrain quite well, either because their families have taken them up this mountain before or because they have

prepared them for the journey. A grade 11 Spanish student, for example, may have a Spanish-speaking parent at home. A grade 9 English student may have university-level professor parents who have encouraged and fostered an advanced level of reading comprehension. These students may take the quickest and most well-trod route to the top. Other students, unfamiliar with the terrain, may take twice as long as they spend hours trailblazing new paths for themselves and others. Other students may spend extra time taking in the views, immersing themselves in their environment, possibly falling down before picking themselves up and eventually finding a way to the top.

Many new assessment policies ask teachers to focus more on the journey, the competencies required to get to the top, and less on the content. In a world of AI chatbots, this kind of authentic assessment can give more weight to the process over the product, demonstrating to students that the value in learning comes from the work it takes to get to the top. It is the journey and not the destination that matters, and that journey will look very different for everyone.

The student who climbs to the top with a full backpack and a guide along the way is going to learn very different skills than the student who starts their journey with nothing, lacks a guide, and must forage along the way. And what about those students who, try as they might, may not quite make it to the top on time but have learned valuable lessons along the way? How do we, as professional educators, honour each individual student's journey and assess these journeys fairly?

Authentic assessment needs to value the journey while focusing on but not overvaluing the destination.

WHAT THE BACKPACK CONTAINS

We all know that some students come to class far more prepared than others. I should have money invested with Bic, Dixon, or Faber, for the number of pencils and pens I buy each year. Beyond the basic supplies, our students are carrying things that cannot be quantified, that we may never know about but that inevitably have an impact on their overall learning journey. Some students will come into their learning journey with the highest quality name-brand gear. Their bags may be well packed with a nutrient-rich lunch and more snacks than they need. Another student may start the journey with a hand-me-down pack with broken zippers and a bruised banana that they grabbed while running out the door. And, of course, we all know the student who doesn't have a pack at all, either because they forgot it or can't afford one. Then, there are the intangibles that may be weighing the pack down: anxiety, learning disabilities and differences, workload, family stress, relationship stress, learning barriers, cultural differences, societal expectations, societal prejudices, and more.

PAUSE FOR THOUGHT

1. Think about a few students in your own classes (or your own children) and what you know they are carrying in their backpacks. How does this impact their experience and learning in school?

2. Think about your own backpack as a student. What were you carrying that your teachers may or may not have known about? How did these things impact your own learning journey?

THE WEIGHT OF A SMARTPHONE

Look at your answers from the Pause for Thought exercise. If you are from a generation born before the early 2000s, chances are good that you did not include in your backpack a smartphone or all the social media implications of having one. You may not have thought to include it in your student's backpack either. But that device, as small as it may be, adds a lot of weight to the load our students carry today.

The Distraction

For many students, smartphones are like having a friend beside them on their journey. It can feel comfortable and safe to have that friend along. The reality, however, is that a smartphone is the kind of friend who sabotages our efforts by distracting us from doing what is good for us. If we're not careful, the smartphone can become the hiking partner who consistently leads us off the path, gets us lost, and causes us to waste countless hours trying to find our way back. It pulls a student off of the task at hand with endless distractions:

> *This looks more fun. Let's go over here and check it out!*
> *You look like you need a break, so let's sit and scroll awhile.*
> *Why go that way when I know a shortcut?*

The Shortcut

Smartphones and technology give students in-the-second access to YouTube videos, apps, calculators, translators, and AI chatbots, all of which provide much of the same information we teach in our courses. The question we educators must ask, then, is this: **How do we convince our students to go on this journey when they have access to thousands of photos of the view at the top?** Why do the work of climbing the mountain at all if I have access to a 24/7, 360° high-definition camera?

The answer—the compelling reason—must be the journey itself. It is more important than ever for teachers to relay the value of the process of the work. Our goal is to help students understand that learning is in the doing, not simply getting the right answer. It is human nature to find the quickest and most efficient way to do something. The quicker students can get their work done, the quicker they can mingle with friends or return to their phones to scroll through social media, text, and play games.

Looking up an answer or having a chatbot do the work is like taking a lift to the top. It is painless and efficient, but ineffective. Learning and growing come from doing and pushing ourselves through the discomfort.

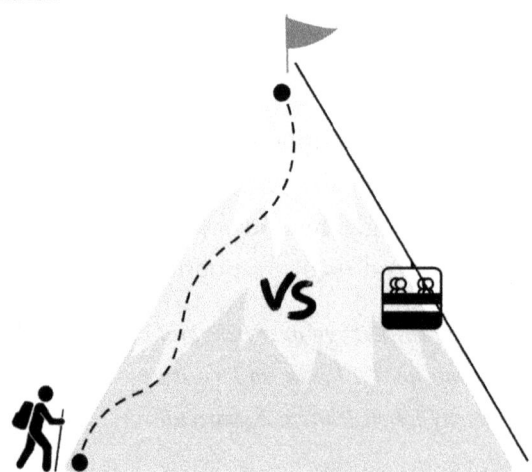

Like many people, I have a love–hate relationship with hiking. Getting to the top is hard! Going up and working our burning muscles is painful and, at times, absolutely no fun. In the worst moments, I question my fitness and my sanity, fighting the urge to turn around and go back. I always hope there are good views to take in along the way to make the struggle of sucking in oxygen a little less painful, but sometimes the payoff for all that effort can only be found at the summit. So, why do I and so many others take to the trails when we know our bodies would be far more comfortable curled up on the couch watching Netflix?

We do it because we know it is good for us, and we know that pain is temporary. We do it because the views at the top are usually (if not shrouded in fog) spectacular. We do it because we want to prove to ourselves that we *can* do it. We do it because things look and feel better when we earn them. We do it to stretch our limits. And after reaching the summit and making it safely back to the trailhead, many of us wonder, *What else I can do?*

This metaphor applies to all kinds of challenges we bring to our students. A difficult math problem? Sure, the AI on our phones is capable of solving it in seconds, but only a student who can push through the pain of struggling and failing will feel the satisfaction of getting the right answer and begin to understand what they are capable of. A student who struggles to research and write a well-formatted history essay that can be written by ChatGPT will know the feeling of elation that comes with writing the last word and will understand that they are capable of doing it again.

When we compare two students, one who took the shortcut and one who pushed themselves through the climb, we know which one will be stronger at the top—and on the *next* mountain.

Our job is to convince our students that the journey of learning is worth the effort. For their long-term success, it is more important than ever that we **stress the *why* over the *what*.**

HOW MUCH DO YOU VALUE THE LEARNING?

Just when I think I understand how students are using and abusing the tech, they show me something new.

About two-thirds of the way through my grade 11 Spanish course, my students were applying their previously learned knowledge on a four-page work booklet. One of my students, let's call her Sara, jumped up from her seat and turned in her sheets. Students handing in work is pretty normal, but Sara handing in the sheets at all, let alone a full class and a half early, was very suspicious. When I asked her what she had just handed in, she proudly responded, "The worksheets," then went back to her desk to chat with her friends. I went to check on how "complete" her work booklet was, and to my surprise, she had indeed finished it, and with more attention to detail than I had ever seen from her. Also very suspicious. I had only just handed it out at the start of class, so either Sara had turned a new leaf and had been studying much more than normal, or something else was up. Knowing Sara well, I suspected the latter. That is when I saw her good friend staring down at her lap and then writing her own responses on the sheets. I asked to see the not-so-well-concealed phone. Knowing they were busted, Sara and her friend gave me the phone.

I was not surprised to see a photo of another booklet completed with answers. I was, however, shocked when Sara said to another student, "Señorita Green just found our group chat."

What I later found out was that one of the stronger students in the class had breezed through the work booklet and, under peer pressure, had taken photos of their completed work, which was then shared with a large group chat. This work booklet was worth a paltry five marks. The point of completing it was to prepare them for a unit test. I had thought that by making the work worth something, I was ensuring students would complete the assignment. Oftentimes, these completion marks, while worth very little, helped to boost a student's grade. But, as has been proven time and time again, external rewards that we think motivate can end up having the exact opposite effect.

As I stood there holding the phone, I could see the students all waiting for my reaction.

Now, I ask you, how would you have reacted in this situation? You have probably undoubtedly faced a similar situation already.

I thought about it. Then I sighed, shook my head, and handed the phone right back. "If you want to use this to copy another person's learning, go ahead." I was disappointed, and I let them know that. I also let them know that the work booklet would no longer be worth anything. If they wanted to do the work, they could. If they wanted to write down another person's answers, they could. They could also decide not to do it at all.

When I think back on it, I am not surprised. As a student, I am sure I took the opportunity to copy a few answers from friends. We are human. It is in our nature to find the most efficient way to get work done. After the wheel was invented, no one carried anything they didn't have to. With smartphones and in-the-moment ways to share information, of course, our students are going to seize any opportunity to get their work done so that they can get back to doing more enjoyable things. That is why it is so important to stress the journey over the destination and to do that at the start of the course.

Now, when students ask me if these sheets are worth anything, I am honest in my response.

"Are they worth anything? Well, that depends."

"On what?"

"On how much you value learning."

PURPOSEFUL LEARNING: STRESSING THE WHY OVER THE WHAT

I have heard many educators say that they shouldn't have to convince their students to learn or have to put on a show to get their students to invest in their education. I don't disagree, but when I consider what it takes for me to devote time and attention in a professional development event, I know that I am far more invested when I am reminded of the reasons I am attending and whether the person delivering the information is engaging.

The *what* of this book is written in the title: to better understand how learning is changing in the era of smartphones and technology.

The *why* (to name a few) is that we recognize that smartphones and the rate of technology are impacting education and student learning. We know that we are already behind when it comes to how we are approaching it. We also know that by putting in time with professional development, we may gain new ideas or be inspired by colleagues who are investing that same time and attention in their careers. We don't always acknowledge the value of getting together with colleagues who are expressing the same concerns and experiencing the same challenges. The truth is, it's helpful if for no other reason than to know that we are not alone.

Educators are aware of the hidden curriculum within our lessons and assignments; for example, the hidden curriculum of assigning a group project could contain skill building of conflict management, collaboration, and accountability. To help our students understand the *whys* of our course, we need to unhide the hidden curriculum. We must help them see *all* the learning and benefits they can take away by investing their time and effort in the class.

Why Stress the *Why*

I don't love working out, but I know that it is good for my overall health. If I focus on what I need to do—go for a run, lift weights, eat healthfully—I lose motivation. But when I remind myself why I am doing it—to potentially live a longer, healthier life, be able to do and access more outdoor activities, feel good in my clothes, feel better at the end of the day, sleep better at night—I find myself lacing up my shoes and heading out the door.

Why is simply more motivating than *what*. If we can remind our students why they are doing something, be it a full course or an activity within the course, they will inevitably be more invested. They'll be even more invested if they write out their own whys and reflect on them in the middle and at the end of the course.

When focusing on the why, we must stress the specific outcomes that will occur when students actively engage in the course or activity. Returning to our mountain metaphor, the setup may sound something like this: We are going to climb to the top of this mountain, and while I know that you could access the pictures at the top or choose to take a shortcut, you should know that in doing this journey yourself, you will strengthen your muscles, be fitter, build your outdoor skills, learn more about yourself, experience new things, understand the terrain, have a better appreciation for the land, and be a much stronger individual with a sense of pride for what you have accomplished.

We cannot just expect our students to want to learn. Even if they *do* want to learn, the distractions pulling at their attention are intense. Smartphones are chief among those distractions, and simply telling your students not to use their phones or instilling consequences in the class is often not a sustainable solution, in part because those rules do nothing to impact their phone use outside the classroom. As educators, we must help students learn to make the right decisions now and in the future. To do that, we have to convey the importance and outcomes of actively engaging in and doing the process work themselves rather than relying on their phones.

STRESSING THE *WHY* AT THE BEGINNING OF THE COURSE

Example: Spanish 9 (Overall Course)
- You are taking this course to better your Spanish speaking, listening, and writing skills so that you will be better able to interact in the Spanish-speaking world.

- You are taking this course so that when you travel to a Spanish-speaking country in the future, you will be able to converse with the locals, which will make your experience more immersive.
- You are taking this course to build your collaboration skills by working with other students to enhance your and their Spanish-language abilities, which will help you to become a better collaborator in any future employment.
- You are taking this course to expand your knowledge of the customs and cultural traditions in Spanish-speaking countries in order to be a well-rounded citizen of the world.

Activity Example: Listening Assignment

By engaging with this assignment, you will strengthen your Spanish-language listening skills, build your vocabulary, and be able to better understand how to talk about yourself with others.

Example: English 9
- You are taking this course in order to strengthen your writing, research, and comprehension skills, which will have a positive impact on all future courses.
- You are taking this course in order to understand a variety of ways in which to communicate your thoughts and opinions to diverse audiences.
- You are taking this course in order to build your collaboration skills by working with other students to enhance your and their English-language abilities, which will help you to become a better collaborator in any future employment.

Activity Example: Creative Writing Paragraph Writing Assignment

By engaging with this assignment, you will strengthen your descriptive writing skills and better understand how to relay your ideas while capturing the attention of your audience.

PAUSE FOR THOUGHT

1. Using the stems below to get you started, try thinking about a few *why* statements you could use on your own course syllabus.

2. Using the stems below, or some of your own, choose an assignment or activity that you give to your students in class and think about a why statement you could add to the top for your students to read before they begin.

Stems to Get You Started
- You are taking this course in order to . . . so that . . .
- At the end of this course, you will be able to . . . , which will provide you with . . .
- This activity will help you to . . .
- By engaging in this activity, you will . . .
- By participating in this activity, you will . . .

Remember to focus on the skills they will build and how those skills will help them in the future.

TRADING CLASSICAL ASSESSMENT FOR AUTHENTIC ASSESSMENT

Classical assessment practices have been built on the idea that society is a meritocracy, that an individual's success depends on that person's talents, abilities, and effort. This could work if everyone were to have an equal starting point: the same tools, the same abilities, and the same path to take. A student who can get up the mountain the quickest may have not necessarily learned much or grown their abilities at all. A student who takes a little longer than others, spending more time in a certain area, may have taken a more difficult route and had to overcome bigger obstacles to get to the top. A student who didn't quite make it to the top, a perceived failure when looking down from above, may have learned far more than others and consider their achievement a victory.

Authentic assessment should examine each student's individual learning journey, taking into account their unique starting and end point, obstacles faced and overcome, and value it based on a case-by-case basis. We cannot always have eyes on all students, and we cannot know everything that is impacting their journey. Therefore, authentic assessment cannot happen unless the student is involved in the overall assessment of their learning journey.

CHAPTER 5

AUTHENTIC ASSESSMENT INVOLVES THE STUDENT

The pandemic demanded flexibility from teachers and allowed for a lot of accommodations when it came to student assessment. It was during this time that I felt emboldened enough to try something I had never done before and let students weigh in on their final grades. Letting students in on a final assessment reflection and interviewing them at the end of the term gave me insights into what each student was dealing with during this time, how COVID was impacting them, how different strategies such as online learning and longer in-class lesson time was influencing their learning, and how their overall mental and emotional health had been impacted. I asked questions and learned things about my students that I never had before. The experience completely changed how I approach my teaching and assessment practice.

In this chapter, I am going to share the assessment strategy that has helped me and my students. I am not writing this to convince you that what I am doing is the best assessment strategy for all teachers or students. I am sharing this because I have found that it works for me; it has made me more confident with my grading, and it has made my final year-end assessments a process I honestly look forward to. That's something I cannot say was the case in the past.

START OF COURSE: THE BUILDING BLOCKS OF CO-CONSTRUCTION

"A student's final grade will be determined after a thorough course reflection and mark defence, in consultation with me."

On the first day of class, when I am going over my course syllabus, I explain how the final grade is determined. Many are surprised and confused. I explain that agency in their learning does not mean they will simply grade themselves; it means that during a one-on-one interview, they will need to provide a final reflection and mark defence that outlines the final percentage they feel they deserve and why. I will still be marking their work, and they will still see an overall grade in the grade book, but that grade will not necessarily represent their final percentage. It is simply a piece of evidence.

After some initial rumblings and inquisitive looks from my students, I explain my reasons, often using the mountain analogy. I want them to understand from the beginning that while I will be joining them, the learning journey and what they take from it will be in their hands.

We can teach all we want, but it is up to the student to do the learning. This is a symbiotic relationship in which the outcome will be co-constructed.

CREATING A PORTFOLIO

One of the first tasks my students engage in is creating a portfolio. Working on their portfolio at the beginning of the course lets them know that I take their personal learning journey seriously, and so should they. It also allows me to get to know my students and their individual learning habits at an early stage.

How you get your students to create their portfolio, and the platform you use, will be different for everyone. I am fortunate to work at a school with access to technology and computers, so I have my students create their portfolios on a digital platform that can be accessed throughout the semester (a slide deck or website). However, there is no reason why a portfolio cannot be created and kept in the classroom on paper. As long as the students have access to it and can periodically add materials to their portfolios throughout the course, any platform you use can work to provide evidence of their learning.

Reiterate that the purpose of the portfolio is not only to track their progress and store their work, but that it will also eventually serve as a crucial piece of evidence of their learning journey in the course and be used in their mark defence. I personally have had to create portfolios in courses I have taken over the years, only to find that the considerable effort I put into the portfolio's creation served no final purpose other than self-reflection. As a teacher, I understand the value of self-reflection; however, time is also a valuable commodity. If something is taking up time without an understood and relevant purpose and is seen as busywork or to tick an administrative box, students will resent the time they need to put in, and the value in self-reflection will be lost.

Portfolios, when used properly, are an effective tool for self-reflection. They allow students to engage with their own learning progress throughout the course, better understand their areas for improvement, and be proud of their areas of growth. They allow students to see just how much they have learned and accomplished. When asked how a course went or what was taken away from a class, it is too easy for students to respond with, "I don't know. We didn't really do much." This kind of response can frustrate teachers and parents alike. Even more damaging, it can be a narrative that the student starts to believe.

A portfolio of work that summarizes the learning journey throughout the course provides evidence that the students did, in fact, complete many assignments in class and have learned many new things. I have witnessed many skeptical students respond in surprise when reviewing and reflecting on their learning and growth in a course, giving value to the portfolio, empowering the student, and providing a needed sense of validation to the teacher.

Setting Up a Learning Journey Portfolio

About Me: a section for students to write a little about themselves, their interests, extracurriculars, etc.

Student/Learning Reflection: an area for students to reflect on their learning interests and styles

Potential Questions

- What parts of school do you enjoy?
- What parts of school do you find challenging?
- List three things you enjoy doing outside of school.
- What is life like for you outside of school?
- Why have you chosen to take _____?
- What are your goals with the course?
- How do you hope to apply the skills and knowledge you learn in this course outside of school?
- What about learning _____ do you enjoy?
- What about learning _____ do you find challenging?
- What areas in _____ do you feel confident in?
- What areas in _____ do you feel need the most work?
- Describe your study and work habits.
- What kind of feedback helps you learn?
- List three learning goals you have for yourself in this course.
- List three personal goals you have for yourself this year/semester.

Technology-Specific Questions or Area for Phone Contract

Student self-evaluation of course competencies and skills: a section where students can rate themselves about where they feel they are, as they start the course, in specific areas. The intent is to come back to this section at the end of the course and rate themselves again to see how their skills have advanced and to use that information as evidence in their mark defence. It is important to make this section simple with the use of student-friendly language.

EXAMPLE—SPANISH 10

	Emerging (Level 1)	Developing (Level 2)	Proficient (Level 3)	Extending (Level 4)
Reading in Spanish				
Writing in Spanish				
Speaking in Spanish				
Listening to Spanish				
Class participation				
Class focus				
Time management				
Collaborating with classmates				
Completing assignments on time				
Personal at home study time				

INITIAL STUDENT CONFERENCES, BUILDING RELATIONSHIPS, AND GIVING THE PORTFOLIO VALUE RIGHT AWAY

After students complete the initial setup of their portfolios, I set aside time to meet with them one-on-one for short conferences. While the class works on a project or assignment that doesn't require my constant supervision, I hold these conferences just outside my room, where I can still be aware of what is going on inside the room.

Over a span of weeks, sometimes going late into the semester if needed, I get to know my students as learners as we review their portfolios together. I want them to know I have eyes on their portfolios and will continue to review their work throughout the course. While these meetings take time, the return on investment has been more than I ever expected. In the first few weeks of the course, I learn things about my students that would have taken me (and used to take me) until near the end of the semester to discover. If you take one thing away from this book to enhance your practice, let it be one-on-one conferences!

The initial student conference averages five to ten minutes and can provide insights into who my students are, what they like and dislike, what takes up their time outside of school, what they are passionate about, how busy they are, how they learn, what they struggle with, and more. This one-on-one time with a teacher is something that some of my students may never get in other classes. The intimacy of these conferences leads students to relay important information they may otherwise have kept to themselves. I am not advocating that teachers become counsellors; however, some of these conferences have led to me either setting up meetings with counsellors or encouraging students to advocate for themselves. The nature of these conferences also allows me to speak honestly and frankly with students about their in-class focus, conduct, phone use, or other issues I see arising. As a result of these interviews, I have better relationships with students and find that classroom management is a much smoother affair.

Information from student portfolios can lead the discussion and questions, but even if you are not having your students create portfolios, these conferences are still extremely valuable, and there are many questions you can ask to begin building relationships.

Initial Student Conferences

1. Start by asking students how they are and how the class has been going so far.
2. If you have their portfolio, open it up and make some comments/general observations about responses or certain things the student included. This will often lead to casual conversation.

- You could ask students the following:
    - Tell me what life is like for you right now. How busy are you?
    - What are you like as a learner? Tell me about your learning style.
    - What parts of school do you find the most challenging?
    - What are you passionate about?
    - Is there anything you particularly struggle with when learning _____?
    - Tell me more about your IEP (Individual Education Plan).
    - How are your organizational skills?
    - What are your study habits like?
    - Is there anything you think I should know that will help me when teaching you?
    - How are you planning on achieving your learning goals? How can I help you to achieve your learning goals?

Taking a few minutes to let students know that I genuinely want them to develop better habits—for class and for life—makes a huge impact. One-on-one conversations build relationships and make students more accountable. As a result of these conferences, I have initiated different seating plans because students were able to privately relay that a friend sitting next to them is too distracting, but they don't know how to say it or move seats. I have learned interesting things about my students that have resulted in how I teach or address them. I have reached out to counsellors, administrators, and parents when required, and I have become a more understanding and patient educator. I am often pleasantly surprised by how well students know themselves and recognize when they are doing things that do not help their focus or learning. Sometimes, they just need someone to call them on their behaviour in a genuinely caring way.

Holding initial conferences with students has made such a positive difference in all regards that I question why I didn't start doing it earlier—and why new teachers are not guided to engage in this practice. I believe that if schools implemented a start-up week dedicated to initial student conferences, then anxiety levels for students and teachers would decrease, classroom management would be less stressful, and the overall atmosphere of belonging and community would improve. Again, if you take one thing away from this book to implement with your own teaching practice, please let it be this!

END-OF-COURSE REFLECTION, MARK DEFENCE, AND STUDENT CONFERENCE

At the end of the course, students have a full class period to complete a personal learning and assessment reflection. This is usually one of the last and most important assignments they will do for the class (and themselves), and it has replaced any final exam I might have given. I reiterate the importance of this exercise by reminding students that it can impact their final grade. The information they provide will be discussed in a final exit interview for the course. I

also stress the *why* of the exercise by saying, "You are engaging in this course reflection and final assessment in order to have a better understanding of how far you have come, how much you have learned, and how much you have grown since the beginning of the course. This will help you to have a better understanding of yourself and reveal areas of strength as well as areas for future development. When we take time to reflect, we can understand ourselves better."

Student Learning and Assessment Reflection

Your assessment reflection should take into account the following:

Think about where you began and where you are now…

- How have you grown?
- What skills have developed?
- How have your skills developed?
- What areas of the course did you struggle with or find challenging?
- What obstacles or challenges did you overcome?
- What could you personally have done differently to enhance your _____ learning/skills?
- What are you able to do now that you could not at the beginning of the course?
- Think about your learning levels as they relate to the learning competencies/skills of the course. In what areas do you feel you are emerging, developing, proficient, or extending?
- What are you proud of?
- What skills would you like to keep working on, or what do you want to learn more about?
- What have you learned in this course and about yourself as a result of this course?

Please take time to reflect on these questions before beginning to write your response. Do not write what you think I (as your teacher) want to hear. As this is your learning journey, be honest with yourself.

Learning Journey—Student Response

1. In the space below, write a well-written paragraph that reflects on your learning journey in this course. Use some of the prompts above to help and guide you.
2. What specific areas or skills do you feel that you need to work on and further develop?
3. How are you planning on continuing your learning journey? What are you still hoping to further explore and find out more about?
4. Describe your work and study habits during this course.
5. How did technology (computer/phone access) impact your learning during this course? This can be in both positive and negative ways.

Course-Specific Prompts

Example—Spanish 10

When you reflect on your learning journey in Spanish, think about the following:
- what you have learned about the language
- how your skills have developed, specifically with the language—sentence structure, verb conjugation, vocabulary, understanding, etc.
- how your speaking and listening skills have developed (Think about the guided readings, partner talk, and listening activities we did together.)
- your understanding of the countries, people, and culture (Think about the culture days, the stories we listened to, and the videos watched in class.)
- what you learned about yourself

The above is an example of general questions and prompts to get students thinking and reflecting on their journey throughout the course and give agency to their learning. I often include course-specific questions that include references to assignments and activities we did, to encourage and guide them to provide specific examples and individual details in each response. Below, you will find real examples of student responses.

Student Response Exemplars

Student A: Spanish 10 Reflection

I came into Spanish 10 knowing the basics I learnt in grade 9. I was hoping to learn more about sentence structure and get further into speaking the language without having to relate it to English in my head. This year, my most noticeable growth in learning was being able to speak, write, and communicate using the basic sentence connectors and words we learned throughout the course. I now understand how to make connections such as more or less, and better or worse, which helps me speak about things in further detail. I am proud of my understanding of conjugating verbs. At the beginning of the year, I was a lot less confident in paragraph writing, mainly because I wasn't always able to conjugate the verbs to the correct gender and plural or singular form. I am proud of my pronunciation and speaking because I am now fairly confident in the fact that I could travel to a Spanish-speaking country and make my way around with the Spanish I have absorbed this term. I plan to take Spanish 11 next year and continue Spanish throughout the rest of high school. I think learning more about the language has made me realise how much fun it would be to travel and apply it to everyday speaking. This course has inspired me to eventually become conversationally fluent in the Spanish language.

Student B: English First Peoples 12 Reflection

At the start of this course, I did not know how to properly format an essay, I could not write a proper intro paragraph, and I had minimal knowledge of Indigenous culture. Throughout the class, I had the opportunity to practice and improve my writing skills, particularly writing formal introductions. I now know how to properly format essays and cite all of my sources correctly. My understanding of Indigenous culture has improved drastically, and I had the opportunity to do my own research on Indigenous carving. I think this helped broaden my knowledge of Indigenous people and gain a new understanding of the importance of visual arts to Indigenous culture. One of the First Peoples' Principles of Learning that I stood by was: *Learning involves patience and time.* In this class, I learned to be patient with myself and understand that learning is a process and does not always come quickly. I have grown not only in knowledge but also in my ability to speak to peers and have discussions. I pushed myself to lead our lit circles and contributed all that I could to our discussion groups. I often found it challenging to manage my time with a large stream of assignments, but I overcame this by using my time in and out of the classroom more effectively. I am proud of my final project, and I'm proud that I picked a topic that really interested me and got a deep understanding of that topic. I would like to continue to develop my reading and comprehension skills as well as my ability to speak in front of the entire class rather than just in small groups.

MARK DEFENCE

While the wording *mark defence* can sound intimidating, I have personally found that when students understand it, they become more active, rather than passive, in the assessment process. For me, the mark defence requirement has provided better overall engagement, as students must prepare, with evidence, why they feel they have earned a final grade percentage for the course. There is value, learning, and serious self-reflection in the creation of the defence. The intent of this exercise is not to put students on the defensive; in fact, the goal is just the opposite. Any sports coach will tell you that a good defence leads to a good offence. Being proactive usually provides better results than having to be reactive. I also believe that advocating for oneself is a valuable life skill that students do not often have the opportunity to harness in school.

The mark defence is a way for students to take ownership of and accountability for their learning. Students reach this point of the final assessment process after they have completed their reflections.

When thinking about what their final grade in the course should be, students are encouraged to take the following diagram into account.

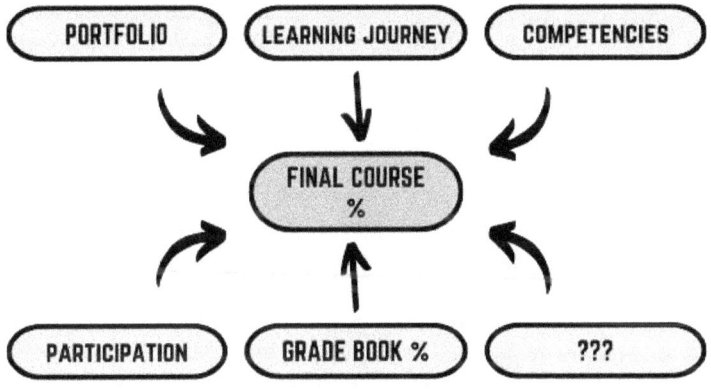

Before students begin the process, we have a class discussion about each of the items students need to consider when arriving at their final percentage. They are guided to think about what the portfolio conveys about their learning and habits, their overall learning journey in the course—where they began with their knowledge and skills and where they are now—how their learning reflects the course competencies, their overall participation with peers, discussions, and class activities, the grade book percent, and finally, the X-factor indicated by ??? on the flowchart.

The ??? will be individual to each student. As the unknown factor, it is the thing that most teachers never consider. It could be anything from the extra work, study, and reading a student put in outside of the course; the effort a student put in while juggling work, a heavy course load, or extra-curricular activities; an obstacle or struggle they had to overcome; the extra time or tutoring they put in to understand a certain concept, or any other number of things that are rarely considered when assigning a final grade.

Students also need to provide a work-habit suggestion and a well-written justification for that work habit, as well as include ways in which to improve those work habits in the future. While it is often this area that produces some interesting conversations, I have found that most students are honest and realistic about their work habits.

Students write their final grade in an area that says, "Final Grade Suggestion." It is important to let students know that the grade will be considered by the teacher and discussed during the final exit conference; it is not a given. If a student's final grade suggestion is different from the final gradebook percentage, they must provide an explanation.

STUDENT EXIT CONFERENCE: INCORPORATING STUDENT VOICE

With the portfolio, final course reflection, and mark defence complete, it is time to move to the final and most important step of the student self-assessment process: the exit conference.

Much like the initial conferences, during this time, students meet with me individually, usually in the hallway just outside the classroom. We go over their submissions and settle on a final grade together. During these conferences, I have my final gradebook open and input the student's final work habits and grades at that moment.

I usually plan for these conferences to take place during the final days of the course. They tend to take longer than the initial meetings, around ten to twelve minutes, which means that if I have thirty students in a class, it can take four or five hours to meet with every student. With that in mind, I plan for a full week of one-on-one exit conferences when the class period is an hour long.

I have heard all the concerns from other teachers: not being able to fit in all their course content, the time commitment, and the lack of a final exam. This style of assessment is not for everyone. It may take a huge adjustment in practice, and yes, it can be difficult to keep students focused in the classroom when they know their course is all but complete. In my ideal school, much like having an introductory week of get-to-know-you student conferences, there would be a final week of final reflection conferences for all courses. Until this becomes the norm, if you choose to conduct exit conferences, you will also likely need to create a plan for keeping the other students occupied in class while you meet with the one in the hallway. Depending on the grade level, I usually direct my students to use the class time as a study or work-completion block, I bring in board games, the class votes on a movie to watch, or I bring in a teacher-on-call to run other activities. Honestly, it would be much easier to have a final week of coursework, a final project, or a final exam, but having done this for the past few years, I know that the students (and I) get far more out of the exit-conference experience. The planning can be a pain, but I will never go back to my old assessment ways. I believe that once you try it, you won't either.

Student Exit Conferences

1. Start by asking students how they are doing or how the end of the semester has gone.
2. As you open their portfolio and bring up their final course reflection and mark defence, ask how they feel the course went overall.

3. Look through their course reflection and find statements that you can comment on. Going over the course reflection will take up the majority of the time.
4. Have a look at their final work habit and grade suggestions and ask them why they feel they have earned that percentage or grade. While it may be written on the sheet, having students talk about this is truly the reason for the conference. If students have not included how they can improve their work habits, this is a good point to have them think about it and explain. This is also a good point for you, the teacher, to comment on the work habits you have witnessed in class and offer suggestions for how students can improve in the future.
5. Together, decide on a final grade.

EXTRA QUESTIONS YOU COULD ASK

- What are you proudest of in this course?
- In which areas do you think you have most improved?
- What was the most enjoyable part of the course?
- Did you achieve your learning goals?
- What did you struggle with the most in this course?
- How are you planning to continue your learning in this area?

TOUGH CONVERSATIONS

For many students, the exit conference will be the first time they have ever had to advocate for themselves. It can be an intimidating process. I try to keep it light by focusing on the positive moments of having the student in class or commenting on work habits that will benefit them in the future. I remind students that this is not meant to be intimidating; it is a collaborative meeting to discuss how the course went overall.

For the most part, students accurately depict with their final grade suggestions. In my experience, when students are hoping for an increase in percentage, they tend to suggest a mark that is 1 to 3 percent higher. In my opinion, the process of reflection, completing a mark defence, and doing an exit conference is worth 1 to 3 percent. Of course, there are always a few optimistic students who suggest a much higher mark than they can defend. When that happens, we have an honest and, at times, difficult conversation. If I disagree with a student's suggestion, I can usually justify meeting them halfway. In those difficult moments, telling a student, "I think I can meet you halfway," results in a relieved smile. Personally, I like putting students on the spot to explain themselves, not because those uncomfortable conversations are enjoyable (they aren't), but because I know how much each student is getting out of the process.

My colleagues have asked, "What if a student wants something way higher than their current grade?" In the years I have been doing this, having taken several hundred students through the process, that has only happened twice. More frequently, in fact, I have experienced students arguing for a lower grade than for something a little too hopeful. For the students who shoot for the stars, I put them on the spot to explain themselves. When they are unable to provide a just argument, we agree upon a grade more accurate of their overall class journey.

There will always be those students who do not value the learning process or who look for a way to get as much as they can out of it—even if they didn't earn it. These exceptions usually occur because of a lack of confidence, insecurity, or embarrassment. In my opinion, it does not make sense to change something that benefits the whole for the exception. When exceptions occur, it is a learning experience for all, including the teacher.

WHAT WE LEARN FROM OUR STUDENTS

I had a student in grade 11, let's call him James, whom I had previously taught in grade 10. Throughout his grade 10 year, James was a difficult student to have in class. In many ways, he was a typical teenage boy, constantly trying to impress his friends and act with much more bravado than I know he had. He was constantly late, often coming in with a lunch he bought, and making his arrival known, as if everyone should be grateful for his presence. Midway through the grade 10 semester, I began fantasizing that James would drop the course as I counted the days until I would never have to teach him again. We all know students like this.

At the end of the course, James and I sat together for his exit conference. To my surprise, he had submitted a well-written course reflection. This is a small portion of his unedited response:

> *To be honest, I think I only really knew the most basic parts of Spanish entering this course like numbers,* hola, adios, gracias, *and all of that stuff. So I think I've progressed a lot since the beginning of Spanish 10. I think I am proud of everything overall with how much more I know now, and I want to keep progressing in Spanish and would one day like to become fluent or at least good enough to travel to a Spanish-speaking country and not struggle with communication with locals. I want to keep working on everything but probably mostly conjugation and things like* beside, above, *or* below *because I struggled with remembering those. In the duration of this course, I have learned a lot about the Spanish language and the cultures surrounding it. I have also learned that I like Spanish and want to become really good at speaking it.*
>
> *My work habits could definitely improve with my procrastination and getting distracted in class but I feel like when I actually get to work I get stuff done fast. I have just recently started working on getting work in on time and I wish I had started sooner but I didn't.*
>
> *I feel like I deserve a higher percentage because while I do have trouble focusing, I do really want to learn Spanish and I am interested in the course. I also feel like in the last little while I have had a good turnaround in Spanish and have been working harder while earlier in the term I was struggling*

> *to focus in all of my classes let alone Spanish. Also, all of my missing assignments are from the times I was absent except for the numbers quiz.*

While I had assumed that James would not take the exit reflection seriously, his response was mature and honest. It was not the response of the student I had seen in class, and I told him that. In fact, I think my exact response was, "James, up until reading this, I did not think that you even liked being in Spanish." James had come into the conference with a 74 percent. For his final mark suggestion, he had written 86 percent. I knew I was headed into a tough conversation.

During that conversation, I put James in the hot seat by asking him why he thought he had earned an A in the course (an A is 86–100 percent). A 12 percent increase and entire grade jump was asking a lot. We discussed his attitude in class and ways in which he could improve his work habits. As I did with the majority of my students, I explained that I believed he was more than capable of earning that A, but there were things he would have had to change earlier in the course to have earned it. He did not disagree, and in the end, we settled on a final grade of 78 percent.

The following year, I had James again. That time around, with a little more maturity, he was a very different student. He still wore an armour of bravado around his friends, but he handed in more of his work on time, was able to focus better, and generally participated well in class. His habit of not coming to class on Fridays, however, caused him to miss many cultural assignments and projects that I normally reserved for that day.

At the end of Spanish 11, James had an 80 percent going into the final exit conference. This is a small portion of his unedited grade 11 course reflection:

> *My learning journey in Spanish 11 has been pretty good overall. I have gotten better at being able to decipher the definition of words even when I don't know the direct definition of them.*

I've also gotten a bit better when it comes to getting things done during class or before the deadline despite that being one of the things I struggle with most in school. I think the main thing that I struggled with this semester was consistently being able to be in the classroom and paying attention and I also got kind of lost when we got around to the preterite tense of verbs. I was able to figure out what I had missed and learn that stuff when I missed classes or wasn't able to pay attention. I used Duolingo for around half the semester and it really helped me but I eventually lost my streak of doing it daily and fell out of the habit. I have gotten much better at understanding spoken Spanish and also determining what is being said without knowing exactly what every word means using context. I was proud of my ability to glide through the first half of the course with what I had learned during the summer through Duolingo. I want to keep working on my problem with procrastination because that is obviously the biggest problem for me in school. I have improved my Spanish vocabulary significantly since the beginning of the semester and I also learned that I should do my work when assigned.

My work habits weren't the best in any of my courses this year but I feel like I did better than last year overall. Not everything got in on time but when I got to the work I really powered through it. I could still improve my work habits by getting things done when they are first assigned and getting them handed in when I finish them because I forgot to hand in a few things even though they were finished.

I progressed a lot this year and I performed really well on the majority of the tests and assignments. I am hoping to finish with 86 percent. I know that 6 percent is a big jump but I still have more assignments I'm going to hand in after finishing this so my grade will be higher than 79.88.

There I was again with James, having to discuss if he truly felt he earned an A in the course, only that time, based on what I had seen from him, I thought he could be right. But I was not going to tell him that.

During our exit conference, James and I discussed how the class had gone, and I made some comments about the positive changes I had noted from the previous year. Before I could address the 6 percent jump, James said that he knew asking for 6 percent was a lot, but that he was missing a few assignments and planned to get them all in by the end of the week.

I asked him what had caused him to have those missing assignments, and why he had fairly consistently missed class on Fridays.

James thought about it, and I saw something I had never seen before. The suit of bravado armour cracked, and James started to get emotional. After a minute of trying to collect himself, he conveyed that there were times when getting up and coming to school was difficult. It was something he had been dealing with since his grade 9 year, when we returned to in-person learning during the pandemic. His parents were aware of the situation, and he was seeing a counsellor outside of school. Adding to this, he confessed that if he was late on Friday for his first class, he sometimes didn't bother coming in at all because he wanted to avoid the anger from his first block teacher.

For me, it was a lightbulb moment. Looking back on my time with James throughout that course, I was finally able to connect the dots. The information he shared that day offered the kind of insights that can change how a teacher approaches working with a student. But James never would have removed his armour and spoken so vulnerably in class. Sitting with him in the hall that day, I realised I had read him completely wrong. It was a big a moment—for both of us.

I told James that he should be proud of the improvements he had made this year, and then I asked him why getting 86 percent mattered to him. He took a minute to respond, then said that he had never gotten an A in high school before and that it would mean a lot to him. (Now, it was my turn to control my emotions.)

Ultimately, we arrived at a compromise that would satisfy both of us. If he turned in the missing assignments and they were done well, he would earn 86 percent. Otherwise he would finish with 83 percent. It was up to him.

At the end of the final week of the course, my school has a designated day called "curriculum completion." Attendance is usually only mandatory for students in jeopardy of failing. Although he had already secured a passing grade, James walked into my room with *all* of his missing assignments. It was some of the best work I had received from him. After turning in his work, James could have walked out and gone home; instead, he sat down and chatted about school and life for the next hour. Both of us were pleased to discover that when those assignments were factored into his grade, James *earned* 88 percent.

My experience with James has made me a more empathetic and understanding teacher, particularly regarding assessment. There was a time before my assessment practices changed when I would have had a hard date set for work being handed in and been far less understanding. I would have justified my firm stance, believing that my being tough on James would cause him to "learn a lesson." I had seen many of my teachers take this attitude, and for many years, assumed I should too.

When I reflect on my experience with James, and with many other students, throughout the portfolio, learning journey, and mark defence process, I can see many more-valuable lessons being learned. While many of those lessons are for my students, I also get a lot out of the process. I build relationships with my students as we engage in productive discussions that I hope impact their habits in positive ways. I feel less pressure and stress surrounding grades. One of the best aspects of this process, for me, is reading my students' exit reflections and learning what they are taking away from the course. In a demanding career like ours, these student reflections serve as a good reminder of why we do what we do.

In an era dominated by technology, where students engage more with screens than with people and have access to information that can automate their work, it is crucial to implement assessment practices that promote accountability and shared ownership of learning. Putting the focus on the value of the learning journey and providing opportunities for authentic assessment throughout the course helps ensure that students focus more on what they learn along the way—and how far they've come—than simply a final grade.

PAUSE FOR THOUGHT

1. How do you make time to connect with your students in class? What barriers get in the way of getting to know your students better?

2. Are there ways in which you can mitigate those barriers and prioritize student conferencing?

CHAPTER 6

TESTING AND ASSESSMENT IN THE ERA OF SMARTPHONES AND TECHNOLOGY

With the rapid advancement of technology, particularly in the realm of generative AI, students are increasingly relying on these tools for their work and learning. This swift progression has left many teachers feeling "behind the eight ball" when it comes to verifying the authenticity of student work and accurately assessing genuine skill development. In this chapter, we will explore educational practices that can help authentically assess student growth throughout a course, as well as testing approaches designed to address the growing dependence on technology in learning.

If you, like many teachers, conduct tests in your classroom, I invite you to consider how much thought, if any, you've devoted to the following questions:

- Why do you test your students?
- What are the goals of testing your students?
- How do tests impact your students?

- Which outcomes result from your testing process?
- How do you use the results of the tests?
- How does the testing process reflect the learning objectives in your course?

STARTING POINTS AND PROOF OF PROGRESS

The ever-increasing reliance on technology has made it essential to conduct incoming and outgoing diagnostic assessments that provide us educators with information and feedback regarding students' unaided, authentic skills and competencies. I like to think of these as "alone-in-the-woods" assessments. What is a student capable of doing by themselves without the aid of anyone or anything?

Diagnostic assessments are not a new concept. It's common to perform diagnostics at the beginning of a course to determine what students are capable of and in which areas they will require the most guidance. This type of diagnostic is not typically factored into the grade-point average, which can make them seem inconsequential to students who may, as a result, not earnestly demonstrate their knowledge and skill sets. With many education ministries shifting to competency-based assessment, however, there is a higher need than ever for authentic and accurate diagnostic assessment, both for the teacher and the learner, in order to demonstrate students' growth and development over time.

Conducting multiple diagnostic assessments throughout the course that cover the same competencies provides valuable information that can be used as a tool for students when reflecting on their learning journey, creating a portfolio, or submitting a mark defence. More importantly, feedback demonstrates that growth is proof of learning and can boost students' confidence in their abilities.

Creating and Utilizing Unassisted Diagnostics

The goal of a diagnostic assessment should be to provide evidence of a student's current capabilities. It should, therefore, be accomplished without aid. Of course, if an Individualized Education Plan (IEP) has directed the use of specific aids for a student, these aids must be provided and utilized as the IEP prescribes. The capabilities being assessed on a diagnostic should reflect the curricular competencies that will be worked on throughout a course.

As noted earlier, students can treat ungraded diagnostics too casually. Students need to be aware that their initial diagnostic will be used as a starting point for their coursework. The hope is that this awareness will inspire authentic engagement. Aside from that information, students should not be given a prompt or have any insight into what the diagnostic will entail other than the format in which it will be provided. This will ensure a more authentic assessment of their current capabilities. Diagnostics that assess the same competencies must be administered in the same format and allotted the same amount of time for completion.

Example: Written Language Diagnostic

Instructions: Without using a phone or translator, use the Spanish you know, and write whatever you can about the above image. Try to use complete sentences to describe the scene(s). This is a free write. You can write about whatever you like as long as it can be connected to the image. You will have ten minutes to write.

In my classes, I have students write a diagnostic about the same image at the beginning and at the very end of the course. I do not tell them they will be seeing the same image. I also add a very different image at the end of the course for a second free write, allotting another ten minutes to complete. Additionally, students complete diagnostics in listening, comprehension, and speaking. At the end of the course, students receive all diagnostics they have completed throughout the course and, using a provided proficiency scale, evaluate their personal growth and development, comparing where they began to where they are now. They use this information as evidence of learning for their portfolio reflection and eventual mark defence.

When creating the content of my diagnostic assessments, I choose images or prompts that reflect both the competencies and content of the course. I have two major aims for these diagnostic assessments:

1. Students see their growth and build their confidence. I want them to leave class knowing that they have learned something.
2. They provide incentives for students to do the work and build their skills. When students know that they will be required to do unaided assessments multiple times throughout the course, they will better understand that they need to be careful how much they use and rely on technology to aid their work.

An unintended but welcomed outcome of these diagnostics has been that I also get to see concrete evidence of their learning. As many educators will attest, seeing the positive results of the work we have put into helping our students grow and develop can be a much-needed motivational boost at the end of the year.

Student Exemplar—Diagnostic Assessment

Diagnostic: End of Semester #1

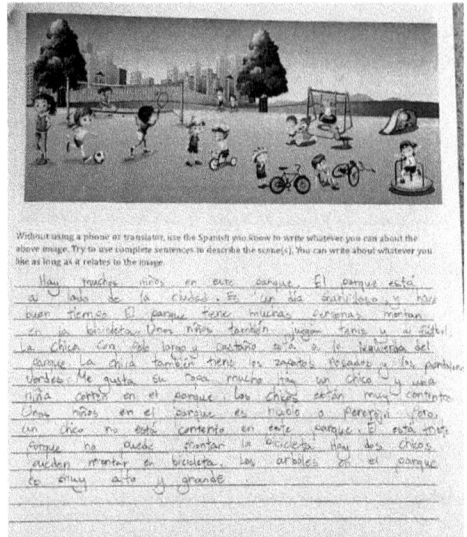

Diagnostic: End of Semester #2

PAUSE FOR THOUGHT

1. Reflecting on diagnostic assessments…What kind of diagnostic assessments have you completed as a student?

   - How were these assessments presented to you?
   - Did you find these assessments helpful with your learning and development? How so?

2. What diagnostic assessments do you have your students complete?

3. What kind of information about your students do these assessments give you?

4. How do you use the information from your student assessments?

5. Do your assessments reflect the competencies and content of your course? If not, how can they?

6. What kind of "alone-in-the-woods" diagnostic assessments can you provide that will demonstrate learning throughout the course?

ASSESSMENT STRATEGIES

A few years ago, I noticed a disturbing trend of an increasing number of students being absent on the day of a test. It did not seem to matter how much time we had spent in class prepping for the test, anxiety prevented many students from showing up. Even among those who showed up for the tests, nerves were high, and some had trouble focusing on or completing the test.

When it comes to testing, the widespread issue of extreme student anxiety has become so common that many high schools have separate test sites. Even with a separate setting option, I still found myself chasing down students for weeks following a test just to get them to take it. I believe there is value in testing and that students need to work on managing their stress and anxiety when it comes to testing and in-class assessments. In fact, as technology allows for more access to information and chatbots give students the ability to have work completed for them, in-class assessments that allow teachers to see what students truly understand and are capable of may need to become more commonplace. How then do we balance the anxiety levels of students with the higher demand for in-class assessments?

Information Being Everything

It should come as no surprise that the more information we have, the less stressed we are likely to feel in most situations. When and where you can, provide students with detailed information surrounding an assessment.

- What material will be on the test?
- What is the test out of?
- How will the test be formatted?

- Which kinds of questions will be on the test? (multiple choice, short answer, paragraph response, etc.)
- How much time will be provided?
- Which tools will be permitted?
- Give guidance on appropriate study strategies for the test.
- Provide possible sample questions.

I have noticed that, for my students, using the same kinds of assessments for each unit lessens their anxiety. My assessments may seem repetitive, but they are predictable. For students with high test anxiety, predictability is one thing I can offer to relieve some of their concerns and help them to refocus on the material.

Alternative Assessments

Open-Peer Assessments

Open-peer assessments allow students the opportunity to work with another student, or group of students, during a test. It essentially allows students to have access to a brain other than their own.

For me, open-peer assessments came about organically. I was teaching a split Spanish 11/12 class with about nine students in Spanish 12. For efficiency's sake, the grade 12s worked at a couple of tables stationed outside of the classroom where I could easily pop in and out of the class and monitor their progress. When it came time for them to write a unit test, I had the option of separating them into spaces where I could not easily see what they were doing, leaving them at the tables where I would need to trust that they would not talk to one another or look at each other's answers a few inches away, or allowing them the opportunity to talk and discuss the test openly. To lessen their stress as well as my own, I decided to tell them that the assessment would be open-peer and that they could work together in groups of three. What I noticed about this process forever changed how I conduct in-class assessments at all grade levels.

Being able to discuss questions and answers with another peer allowed students the opportunity to explain what they knew and why they knew it. They were not simply giving one another the answers. They discussed the questions and agreed on the answer through deductive reasoning. This testing experience also fostered their social skills. As I watched the process, I noticed students positively collaborating, productively discussing different options, questioning themselves, challenging each other, and ultimately, *learning*. It was a light bulb moment for me.

Later, I reflected on why the open-peer assessment had worked so well. Was it simply because those were my mature grade 12 students? Could the process work for any grade level? I decided to try that form of assessment at other grade levels to see if I saw similar results, and I did.

Over the past couple of years, I have tried various forms and different group sizes and pairings to see what works best for the students and for what I want my students to get out of this style of assessment. Here is what I have learned so far.

1. **Pairs are best for this kind of assessment.** Sometimes groups of three are necessary because of odd numbers in a class, but those groups should be well thought out in advance. Often, groups of three will exclude one person from contributing.
2. **Assessment pairs should be organized and assigned by the teacher.** Letting students choose their partner can result in students feeling pressured to pair up with friends they do not necessarily want to test with and can be very exclusionary.
3. **Assessment pairs should be decided on based on in-class effort demonstrated by the students.** Randomly assigning students can result in higher anxiety levels. Students worry

that they will be paired with someone they will end up simply giving the answers to and who will not pull their own weight. I give a lot of thought to how students will be paired up, and I let students know that the pairings will be made by the effort I have seen demonstrated. Students must trust that I will pair them with another student with whom I believe (in my professional judgment) they will collaborate well.

4. **Do not let students know whom they will pair with until the day of the assessment.** Students are very keen to know whom they are going to test with. In the past, I have let students know a day ahead of time whom they would be working with so that they could go over the material in class together and make sure that they each understood the concepts. For the most part, this can work well and result in students teaching each other before the test. It can also result in students dividing up the study material so that they do not have to put in as much work, and (for me) that is not the goal of testing.

5. **Not all testing formats are equally suited for open-peer assessment.** This form of assessment works best with multiple-choice, fill-in-the-blank, and short-answer questions but can work with others.

6. **Even though they are testing with a partner, students are responsible for their own test and do not have to put the same response as their partner.** Students often disagree about an answer. This is a part of the process, and I encourage students to put down the answer they feel is correct because they are all responsible for their own assessments.

7. **Provide alternative options for students who are away on test day.** For students who are absent on test day or who prefer to test by themselves, it is important to provide alternative testing options, such as the opportunity to work with a peer who was also away, the opportunity to write the test with notes for a maximum percentage of 80 percent (more on this

below), or the opportunity to write the test on their own for a possible 100 percent.
8. **An alternative to full open-peer is half-open-peer.** With half-open-peer, students write the test themselves and are then allowed a specific set amount of time (five minutes) to talk at the end of the test to compare, discuss, and potentially change answers.

HIGHER MARKS AND GREATER CONFIDENCE

I love watching my students when they are open-peer testing. The energy in the room is positive and collaborative. Instead of feeling like I am subjecting my students to a torturous, painful, and anxiety-inducing experience, I feel like I am providing them with the opportunity to share their knowledge and understand the benefits of true collaboration. Studies point to the mental health benefits of helping another person, which can include boosting one's self-confidence, self-awareness, and self-esteem. I have witnessed the effects of these benefits firsthand. When open-peer testing, I often see students smiling, laughing, and enjoying the test experience. Marks are higher, yes, and so is student confidence.

Take a look at what my students have to say about the open-peer test format:

- *I like that we are given the opportunity to collaborate with others in the class.*
- *I think it takes some of the stress off. I still feel like I have to study so that I can be confident in my answers, but I like talking them through with another person.*
- *I enjoy the open-peer test format because it relieves a lot of stress on test day. Because we are partnered up with students who put in the same amount of work as us, it helps students and encourages them rather than giving them an excuse not to study.*
- *I think it's a good idea provided partners are thought through and are fair.*

- *Being able to talk to someone else helps me to think things over.*
- *I really like it, being able to work with someone else and use both our knowledge on the subject and be able to help each other makes it a better experience.*
- *It is really helpful to be able to talk through the questions and answers.*
- *It's kind of fun and I like doing the test instead of hating it.*

The number of my students who are absent on test day has decreased significantly since I implemented open-peer testing. Students who previously preferred to test in a separate area or have an IEP that usually guides them to test in a quieter setting often choose to stay in class and test with a peer, even when provided the option to test in a separate setting. I believe this is because the testing environment is more relaxed and creates less tension than a quiet space. To my colleagues who argue that it is important to test in a more classic manner because doing so prepares students for what they will face in many post-secondary environments, I point to the value of open-peer testing that goes far beyond the classroom. Being allowed to discuss questions, share knowledge, ask for help, and work out problems with another peer are collaborative skills that people use in many different work and life situations. It is important to learn to operate in a high-pressure environment; however, the majority of high-pressure situations encountered in life and work require individuals to collaborate with others, and this is a skill set that many now recognize is lacking (perhaps due to technology and smartphone usage) and should be fostered in school wherever and whenever possible.

Open-Book Assessments

When students hear that there will be an open-book assessment, the usual response is a collective sigh of relief. While some students view this as an opportunity to annotate a text and write helpful notes, others feel it is an opportunity to slack off because they think the answers will be there when they need them. For many students, open-book assessments can offer an anxiety-relieving crutch similar to a security blanket. What they may not realise, at least initially, is that an open book can also provide a false sense of security; it is not an excuse to forgo studying.

As they would for any other assessment, students need to prepare for open-book assessments. This preparation, from the teacher's role, means providing detailed context for what the assessment will entail, including topics and length. Students need to understand the amount of time required to sift through texts and binders. The more information teachers provide in terms of what to expect, the less stress students will have going into an assessment, something that is true for all assessments.

Highlight What You Know

Instead of providing a regular test with questions and answers, give a test that asks students to write down as much as they know about the material. You can be more specific and ask students to write down the steps they would use to teach others about the concept. You could also ask them to write as much as they can about why a specific topic is important.

Cheat-Sheet Assessment

Cheat-sheet assessments come with both positive and negative aspects. On the positive side, while students write their notes and prepare their cheat sheets, they are reviewing the material. Limiting the size of the cheat sheet, for example, to an index card, can help students learn to be concise and summarize the important points. Much like the open-book assessment, having some control over what information they bring with them into the test can relieve or reduce test anxiety. On the negative side, unless we sit and watch each individual student write their notes from scratch, we have no assurances that they have done the research themselves and not copied a cheat sheet from a classmate.

Here are some tips for cheat-sheet assessments:

1. The teacher should select a uniform-size note card or sheet for the entire class.
2. Unless a student has been given an accommodation, all notes should be written by hand.
3. Cheat sheets should be handed in with the test.

Ticket to the Test

If you don't want your students to use a cheat sheet, but you want to ensure that they are reviewing the material, you can still have them do the above note-taking activity and direct them to hand in their notecards as a ticket to the test. No note card, no notes, no test.

Another great way to ensure that they are reviewing the material is to create your own fill-in-the-blank outline that has them going over and writing down exactly what you want them to study before the test. This ticket to the test can also include a section that has them relaying how much personal time they have put in reviewing. I find that students are generally honest about the time they have put in. Unfortunately, too often the honest answer is "none." Referring to these sheets can be helpful when students are upset about their test marks or ask why they aren't doing as well as they had hoped in your class.

PAUSE FOR THOUGHT

Reflecting on alternative assessments . . .

- Thinking about your subject area, what are the skills you are most concerned about being diminished by students' reliance on technology? What alternative assessments could you implement to evaluate these skills more authentically?

- How has the increasing use of generative AI impacted students' critical thinking and problem-solving abilities in your course? What forms of assessment could help ensure these skills are still being developed?

- Which core competencies in your subject area do you feel are hardest to assess accurately due to the influence of technology? Which alternative methods could provide a clearer picture of student growth in these areas?

CHAPTER 7

BUILD THE SKILLS

There was a time when I expected that students would come into my class with well-fostered study skills like effective notetaking, time management, critical reading, and the ability to engage in independent problem-solving. As a high school teacher, I assume students learn study strategies in earlier grades with other teachers or at home. However, over the past fourteen years, I have had to lower my expectations gradually, as I've noticed that many students now struggle with these foundational skills, often favouring shortcuts over deep learning practices. With the increasing reliance on technology and quick access to information, most students are lacking the skills, choosing not to use them, or (more likely) getting distracted by more-enticing activities and simply forgetting to study.

Even the best time-management and study strategies, however, are useless if they are not being used. Students in the era of smartphones and technology need to not only learn good study techniques but also develop better study habits and self-regulation skills.

I would be very curious to know if there is a correlation between the decline in studying and the increased use of technology and smartphones. My instincts tell me that this may be the case. How could it not be? Even now, I am actively resisting the urge to pick up my phone, open a new window, and search the internet for my next vacation opportunity, check my email, or head to my favourite online store. As an adult, I have better self-control than a teenager or child, and I *still* find myself picking up my phone and mindlessly scrolling Instagram before becoming aware of the fact that I need to turn my focus back to the task at hand.

So how do we combat the distractions, stay focused, and do the work? It doesn't matter if we're talking about completing an assignment, studying for a test, or writing a book; much of our success lies in our ability to stay on task. I've learned a few hacks that help me. Before I sat down to write this chapter, for example, I set a forty-five-minute timer on my phone and then put it out of sight and out of reach. When the alarm goes off, I will allow myself a brain break, a stretch, and perhaps a quick cup of tea. Then I will reset the timer and get back to work.

One thing that helps me focus on my task is having a clear goal in mind. My ultimate goal is to complete this book and help others understand how learning is shifting in the era of smartphones and technology. My mini goals include writing for ninety uninterrupted minutes today and completing this section. My mini-mini goals include staying focused and not allowing myself to do anything during this time other than either tap on my keyboard or stare at this screen.

I offer this peek into my writing process because it is important to convey just how much it takes for me to do something that I am *motivated* to do. Imagine the self-regulation required for students to stay focused on a task they are *not* motivated to do.

Staying focused takes some serious self-regulation, and that takes specific strategies that I have harnessed because I know they work for me. One of the most important things that we, as teachers, can do for our students is to help them develop time-management strategies that work for them and that they can use as a continuing life skill.

STEP-BY-STEP

There is a well-known African proverb that states the only way to eat an elephant is one bite at a time. In keeping with our mountain metaphor, I like to think that the only way to climb a mountain is one step at a time. The point is that seemingly insurmountable tasks, such as studying for a big test or tackling a complicated project, can be less daunting when broken up into smaller parts. We all know this is true. It's why, for decades, English teachers have been breaking down essay-writing steps, science teachers have been demonstrating the scientific method, and math teachers have been hanging posters in their rooms with the order of operations. Breaking down big projects into smaller steps for your students is one way to model an effective time-management strategy. Going one step further and assigning approximate times they should spend on each step is another.

EXAMPLE: Create a general slide presentation (3–5 slides in total).

STEP 1: Decide on your topic (5–10 min).

STEP 2: Research and gather information on your topic (30–60 min).

STEP 3: Create a slide presentation: Input information, gather images, and format the presentation (45–60 min).

STEP 4: Refine your presentation (10–20 min).

STEP 5: Share your presentation (5–7 min).

Total time allotted: (1.5–2.5 hours)

Sharing approximate times that an assignment should take is good for both the procrastinators and the perfectionists in your room. It can serve as a challenge, a checklist, and a reminder to stay focused and to keep progressing with a destination in mind. As students become more familiar with breaking down steps, you can have them do this themselves by providing a template and asking them to allot approximate amounts of time that they feel will be required for each step.

Goal Setting Never Getting Old

As I mentioned above, one of my personal strategies for accomplishing any project, big or small, is to set a goal and then break down that goal into many mini goals. If you are a goal setter, ask yourself where, when, and who taught you to do it. I learned the power of goal setting from high school basketball coaches who made my team write our individual goals on note cards at the beginning of the season. It is a practice I have consciously and subconsciously continued to do my whole life, and it is something that I just assume everyone does. As I have learned from many of my students, that assumption could not be more wrong.

You may be asking, *what does goal setting have to do with learning in an era of smartphones and technology?* The answer: everything.

Over the years, I have witnessed an increasing apathy in students when it comes to getting started on assignments. I believe this is due in part to the fact that many of them legitimately feel overwhelmed when faced with work to do. They would rather escape by distracting themselves with games or scrolling through social media than get started. I know that I am not the only teacher to notice this trend, and I believe it is our responsibility to help our students find tactics that can help them get motivated to do their work.

Teaching students about setting goals can help them to see the top of the mountain and give them a starting point to break down the steps it will take to achieve the goal. A goal can be as small as completing an assignment, as large as getting a certain grade in the course, and as personal as working to speak up or otherwise participate in class. Breaking down those goals into smaller steps serves two important functions:

1. It makes the larger task seem less daunting and more doable.

2. Completing small goals provides students with the instant gratification that social media has trained them to crave.

Goal-Setting Steps

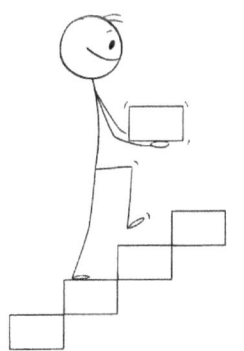

1. Select your main goal.

2. State how long you believe it will take to achieve that goal.

3. Set a date or an estimation of how long it will take to achieve your goal. This is a crucial step in the process of achieving a goal, as the deadline serves as a reminder to keep the goal-setter on track. Not achieving a goal in a desired time does not mean the goal-setter has failed but offers an opportunity to reflect and reset.

4. Segment your main goal down into specific mini-goals—the steps needed to climb to the top of the goal mountain.

Student Example:

Main Goal: Complete a 1500–2000-word short story.

Timeline: 1 Week (7 Days)

Mini-Goals (steps):

- Brainstorm ideas.
- Start writing.
- Write every day for at least 20 focused minutes.
- Write 250 words a day.
- Revise and edit the story.
- Hand in the story.

Goal setting is something you can have your students do in their portfolio at the start of the course. You might set goals together when you assign a large project, or you may have students create their goal-setting steps at the beginning of all assignments. Modelling the process for them and providing templates they can use and adapt throughout the course equips them to practice this essential skill.

Goals cannot be set for others. Goals are personal, and if they are to be achieved, they must be set by the individual. As much as I would like to have every one of my students set personal goals, I know that only a few may choose to do this. Even fewer will make it a lifelong habit. That's okay. By modelling this skill and giving them the opportunity to practice goal setting, I am, at a minimum, helping them understand its value. It's up to them to build on the skill and use it to their advantage long term.

PAUSE FOR THOUGHT

1. What strategies do you use to keep yourself motivated and focused when working?
2. Have you discussed focused work strategies with your students?

3. Choose a few main assignments or projects that you do in your class and try to break them down into mini steps with allotted times attached.

Small Steps Taking You Places

Setting small goals is something you can encourage students to do whenever they need to focus on a task. It's also a way to help them manage their smartphone use. Before students start to read or work on an assignment, remind them to set a personal goal about how much they hope to accomplish during the time they have. Everyone works at a different pace, so each student's goal should reflect their own expectations. Start small. Tell students that you are going to set a timer for twenty minutes of focused work. Ask them to write down what they hope to achieve during those twenty minutes.

EXAMPLES

Task: Study a novel and answer associated response questions.

Student Goal: Read all of Chapter 2 (10 pages) and then get up to question 3.

Task: Create a slide presentation about a famous poet.

Student Goal: Research, gather notes, and create an introductory slide.

Task: Complete a series of math problems.

Student Goal: Ask the teacher for guidance. Complete three to five problems.

You can encourage students to write their goals at the top of their assignment before they begin to work, give each student a slip of paper to write their goal on, or create a goals-setting outline that students keep in their binders and can build from throughout the course of the semester. Each student should keep their goals somewhere they can see them easily, such as on their desk. Seeing the goals reminds them of what they need to be working on or hope to accomplish. That way, when the students feel the urge to check their phones or get off the task for another reason, they have a visual cue to redirect their focus.

At the end of the class period, ask students to do a quick reflection: *Did I accomplish my goal today?* If the answer is yes, they should give themselves a check mark. If the answer is no, they should write down what they were able to accomplish and reflect on why they were unable to achieve their goal. If students track their progress on goal-setting sheets in their portfolio, they can use them as evidence of their progress and development over time. Goal setting needs to be intentional, individualized, and realistic. It may take some time to guide students to understand and set accomplishable but slightly challenging goals. The practice, though, should help students to stay focused, build work habits they can apply outside of school, and boost their confidence.

Checking off a goal, even a small one, releases dopamine in the brain, which links to positive feelings that make us want to repeat the process. Quite simply, we like checking things off a list, and the more we do it, the more motivated we become to do it again. The simple act of checking our smartphone and social media accounts also releases dopamine, a contributing factor to the addictive tendencies we are seeing in many students today. I am not saying that having students check an item off of their to-do list will change their smartphone habits, but if we can change where that dopamine release is coming from and show them how rewarding accomplishing a personal task can be, maybe we will help them to become more self-directed learners.

EXAMPLE: STUDENT GOALS SHEET

LEARNING AND WORK GOALS NAME:			
DATE	TASK	GOAL	✓

Using stickers or a special stamp, you can reward students every time they accomplish their tenth goal, increasing their motivation to get more done. It may sound silly at the high school level, but even as an adult, I like getting a sticker for a job well done. Collecting stamps or stickers also gamifies the practice. We like rewards. Just think about the stamp or punch you get at the coffee shop or pizza restaurant. We also like to see progress streaks, which is why so many apps are able to lure us back each day.

CREATING A DISTRACTION-FREE AND FOCUSED STUDY ZONE

It says a lot that the latest updates on most smartphones have included settings that allow the owner of the phone to set focused hours for work, sleep, and personal time. Even our technology acknowledges that our smartphones are a distraction! In fact, for most of us, our phones have become the largest distraction in our lives, and yet, as of this writing, schools may have banned smartphones but have not implemented a curriculum, lesson, or class that teaches students how to self-regulate and manage tech-  nological distractions. Maybe this exists somewhere. If it does, please share! All of today's youth (and educators) will be better for it.

One of the best strategies we can teach students in regard to their academic success is how to create a distraction-free, focused study zone. It can be as simple as putting one's phone out of sight when trying to study or work on an assignment. Because self-regulation often works better with clear guidelines and goals in place, we start there. Once students have determined what their goal is and have segmented it into mini steps, they should know what they need to do. The hope is that with a clear plan, they also have the motivation to get the work done.

The next step in empowering students to take control of their study habits is to help them identify their distractions and create a distraction-free zone that enhances their odds of staying focused. If I acknowledge that my phone is a distraction, I can keep it on silent and out of sight when I am trying to focus on work. If I acknowledge that going on YouTube can suck me into a time warp while I watch my favourite celebrity interviews, scroll through fun recipes, and curate interesting videos for my classes, then maybe I can keep myself from opening that search window and going there in the first place.

Self-awareness and self-regulation are essential skills to develop for many aspects of life. Just as understanding the consequences of drinking too many margaritas helps me avoid over imbibing, these skills can also help limit distractions from technology. If I acknowledge that the alcohol and sugar content in a margarita will most likely result in a headache, interrupted sleep, and an unwell feeling the next day, I am less likely to drink it. Knowledge gives us the self-awareness that can empower us to make better decisions. If we choose to ignore the facts, we have only ourselves to blame.

PAUSE FOR THOUGHT

1. Create a list of the personal distractions you had when you were a teenager trying to focus on your work.
2. Create a list of the personal distractions that you currently have when trying to focus on your work—the more detailed, the better.
3. Create a list of the distractions that you think your students have when trying to focus on their work.
4. Compare your above lists and consider how distractions have changed over the years.
5. What strategies can you help students to foster and apply that will help them navigate these distractions?

Having students acknowledge their distractions can give them the information they need to make better decisions for themselves. If they know that having their phone nearby is a distraction that causes them to go on it, and by going on it, they will inevitably open one of their favourite apps or games and spend the next ten, twenty, or thirty-plus minutes not getting the thing done that they should be doing, then maybe, just maybe, they will make the decision that most benefits them. As much as we may want to, we cannot control our students' actions or force them to learn. We can, however, help them to be more accountable for their actions. That is a valuable lesson and a small victory in and of itself.

TIMING IS EVERYTHING

When students tell me they are struggling to understand a certain subject or that they did not do well on a test, I often ask them how long they spent studying or reviewing the material. More often than not, the wide-eyed expression I get in return suggests that my question is amazingly profound. You might think I'm trying to be funny or that I'm being harsh. Neither is true. This com-  mon response from students signifies two things: 1) Many students don't put in any extra effort outside of class, and 2) The idea of studying might not have even occurred to them.

Next, I ask, "Why didn't you study?"

The most common response is that they didn't have time.

Now, I do not disagree that students today are busy with many extracurricular activities, friends, and work. I also do not disagree that these activities are important. I do, however, find it difficult to believe that they don't actually have the time to study. The simple truth is that most of us find the time for the things we value, and I would argue that many students do not value learning. They value getting good grades and achieving high marks, but they do not value the learning that should go into achieving those grades. This is not their fault. It has everything to do with the value society places on achieving high grades. This is also the reason it is important that educators reiterate the value of the learning journey to the top of the mountain or end of the course. The value comes from the skills and competencies students build through the learning experience and not from the content we teach.

When a student tells me that they don't have the time, I ask them if they have fifteen minutes. There is usually a pause, some thought, a funny look, and then a response of, "Well, yes."

Fifteen minutes. We can all find fifteen minutes in a day. If I want to get cheeky with my students, I ask them to tell me how many minutes a day they spend on their phone. Students never want to answer that question because they know, as much as I do, they are spending way too many minutes on their phone, and they can definitely afford to subtract fifteen minutes from the total.

Considering that students today do not feel they have much time and that today's generation struggles with focusing for long periods of time, I often suggest that my students try the Fifteen Minute Study Strategy, or the 15MSS. This strategy may have been inspired by the Pomodoro Technique developed by Francesco Cirillo in the late 1980s. The genius of these two techniques is that they only require short bursts of focused attention. If fifteen minutes seems too long, I ask my students how long they think they can focus. If the answer is eight minutes, then I say to start there.

The rule is that focused study time, however long it is, is completely focused time. No phones. No distractions. Students decide what they need to study, review, or complete; then they set a timer and get to work. When the timer sounds, they are finished. Or, if they feel they have another set in them, they go again. Students have the power to customize their focused study times as needed. The key is making this focused time a habit and to commit to implementing the practice as many days a week as possible. Fifteen minutes, three days a week may not sound like much of a commitment, but that is forty-five focused minutes. Compared to zero, forty-five minutes can have an impact.

In my experience, some students try this and fail to continue. Some never try it. Others try it and find that it works for them. Some have even come back to me and bragged about building up their focused time. This is the beauty of focused study habits over time. It can build the students' capacity for longer periods of focused work time, it demonstrates what can be accomplished in a short, focused period, and it guides students to understand the power of positive habits.

HANGING IN THERE

I have to be honest here. As I write this book, there are less than two months left in the school year, and smartphone management in my classroom has eroded to the point of being almost nonexistent. I practice what I preach, and I have put into play many, if not all, of the strategies written about in this book. While many have worked, nothing has stuck. Last week, as I stood at the front of my room watching 95 percent of my students quietly focus on their phones while I waited to begin the lesson, I contemplated trashing this whole book. But this is the reality of the ongoing smartphone battle. It is not easy. There will be setbacks. There will be frustration. There will be many moments of wanting to give up. To quote the famous cat poster of the 1970s, hang in there. All we can do is keep trying. That's what I did. It's what I'm doing every day.

I took a breath and patiently (more or less) said, "Well, it is obvious that at this point of the school year, certain bad habits are starting to creep back in. This is probably my fault as much as it is yours, and I am sorry. It is obvious that I need to be much better at reminding all of you that your phones are a distraction to your learning, and they need to be turned to silent and put somewhere out of sight. That means they should not be on your desk or in your lap. You can put them in the phone caddy at the back of the room or in your backpack. If the phone caddy is too far to walk, I would be very happy to put them away for you."

At this point, I had their attention, and even the stragglers, seeing their classmates following suit, were reluctantly signing off and putting their phones away. I did have to make a second announcement that good learning habits also, "mean students should not have earbuds in their ears." That was followed by a couple of groans and reluctant compliance.

I made the announcements with an intentioned calm, for the students and for myself. I reminded myself that getting upset about it is only going to impact my health and my relationship with the students. Anger or frustration are not the tones I want to set for my lesson.

When you see students in your classes on phones during your lesson or pulling them out during class, do not take it personally, and do not feel it is your fault. You are doing the best you can. You are trying. We need parents and the rest of society to try with us.

I do not think that parents or members of the general population who are not in a classroom with teenagers understand the smartphone burden that is put on educators. Every day, we put on our armour in preparation for the battle ahead. Over time, it gets heavy. The constant reminders throughout the day to "put your phones away" and "take your earbuds out" are exhausting and deflating, and they are not something with which teachers of previous generations had to struggle. While we should be focusing on delivering a lesson and helping students with educational needs, *our* attention is pulled by the distractions of our students' phones. None of us signed up to be the phone police, but it has unfortunately become a large focus of the teaching profession.

Hang in there. I'll be hanging right beside you.

CHAPTER 8

TEXTBOOK TO TECH AND THE LOSS OF SHARED EXPERIENCE

I graduated from high school in 1998. It was the cusp of the digital era and the information age. My school library had five computers with dial-up internet that provided access to rudimentary online search engines, a research novelty. Students had to put their names on a signup sheet if they wanted some computer time.

Little did I and others of my generation realise that within the next ten years, the card catalogues and Dewey Decimal system we had taken quizzes on to demonstrate our understanding would be considered educational dinosaurs. It is an understatement to say that things have changed. The library, once full of books and individual study carrels, is now called the *learning commons* and is full of computers and collaborative workspaces. Textbooks and teachers, once the keepers of knowledge, have been replaced by the internet.

Over the past twenty years, the internet and information era has dramatically changed the basic foundations of education and caused the learning landscape in the classroom to shift focus from teacher-centred instruction to student-centred learning. While many people praise the deviation from outdated textbooks, rote learning, and standardized testing, the emphasis on individualized learning brings into question the purpose of educational institutions and the potential implications on general society.

TIMES A-CHANGIN'—AGAIN

In the mid-1800s, government education reforms across Canada ensured that education existed in the public realm because "schools existed to serve the political, economic, and social needs of the state and the society." Children who once may have learned from their parents and elders on the farm had increasing opportunities to enter schoolhouse classrooms and learn with their peers. The changes provided an opportunity to instill common moral and societal values on a large scale. Ultimately, the school classroom became an important space to learn alongside others how to be a functioning member of society. Textbooks offered a method of uniform delivery.

In my school today, textbooks seem to have divided teachers into two primary camps: one that values them, and one that is more than ready to throw them into the recycling bin. I hate to say that these camps are defined by age groups, but more so than not, it is the seasoned teachers who defend the use of textbooks in class. And then there are people like me, who, having grown up on the cusp of the digital era and experienced the shift to tech-based resources, truly understand both sides of the argument.

One of the benefits of textbook instruction is that all students learn the same material in the same way and then are tested on that same content. The common source of content provides not only similar cultural experiences and knowledge from a peer-reviewed source but also, theoretically, ensures a level educational playing field. That's not to say that textbooks aren't without issues. Historical and cultural narratives are often controlled by those in power, which means textbook content may be presented through a biased lens that glosses over or completely omits minority perspectives. The truth and reconciliation process in Canada, for example, is actively trying to undo years of indoctrinated colonizing perspectives and beliefs that have created lasting harm on Indigenous populations. Many of these perspectives were taught through textbooks in the education system. The alternative, accessing information online, has opened the gates to multiple perspectives. It has also created a flood of opinionated information lacking critical thought and researched facts.

At the beginning of the new millennium, the digital and information revolution altered how the average citizen could access information and, more importantly, how students in classrooms learn. "Digital learning materials completely overhaul how classes, from pre-K to grad school, are conducted; how students are tested on knowledge; and how teachers fit into the picture." The classic textbook and one-size-fits-all educational style has become obsolete, and the repercussions on educational institutions as well as society are starting to reveal themselves.

In a major pivot on how information is disseminated, the once teacher-centred classroom has become a learner-centred environment, and learning has taken a much more constructivist approach. Harking back to the educational theories of John Dewey and Maria Montessori, education today is pushing towards trends of inquiry learning and the belief that children learn best through personal exploration and experimentation. In a constructivist-dominated classroom, students are "treated like experts who investigate, discover, and construct their own meaning," and the emphasis on specific content learning has been replaced by "the accrual of skills and competencies that will be relevant to their future work."

The digital and information era has changed how individuals in society learn. Curricular content that once ensured large groups of society were learning similar things in a similar fashion—the same texts, novels, playwrights, and poetry—is being replaced by competency skills and place-based curriculum "that is focused on the unique strengths, histories, and characteristics of the local." It is certainly a more modern perspective on learning, but how this seismic shift in education is going to impact society is yet unknown.

The digital and information era has also brought with it social media and the algorithms that target its users. The dangers of this have been discussed in documentaries like *The Social Dilemma* (2020), with some psychologists believing that social media is causing a cataclysmic social divide, the consequences of which we are only beginning to see. While social theorists scramble to explain why societies are seemingly becoming more divided when it comes to political and personal ideologies with digital algorithms that send internet users down dark misinformation holes, one must wonder (I certainly do) if the information age that has inspired a shift from group-focused learning to individual-focused learning has also been an influence.

I have colleagues who are ready to "retire" Shakespeare. During English department meetings, I have witnessed heated arguments about the current relevance of The Bard's work. Personally, I side with keeping Shakespeare as a part of the regular English curriculum, and my vote has nothing to do with the quality of the work. To omit Shakespeare, or any other pillar of the common curriculum, is the loss of a shared experience that explores important universal themes. Today, we are inundated with information. It is liberating to be able to watch, read, or listen to anything we want at any time we want. It can also be isolating. When TV programming was set to specific times and days, we may have had to wait for our favourite program to air the next crucial episode, but we waited *together*. Then, together, we watched the episode and looked forward to gathering the next day by the proverbial water cooler to discuss our thoughts and reactions. In many ways, we have lost that shared experience, and I believe we have lost something undefinable and very important with it.

We are teaching in a time when technology and access to information are advancing and entertainment is increasingly individually selected, viewed, and experienced. As an educator, I can see the benefits of individualized learning as well as the benefits of having more material options to select for in-class content use. In the past, students may have read the same stories or used the same textbook that their siblings or parents used simply because budget limitations prevented other viable options. While the mention of these stories in the house may have been met with eyerolls and comments from parents who groaned that they had to read the same thing when they were in school, it also created a shared experience and potential point of discussion to explore themes, ideas, and opinions. Today, there is little need for students to be reading the same stories that their parents read in school. Information is digitally accessible, and content is less expensive or free, the material options for class use are endless. As a teacher, I find this both exciting and daunting. I love finding the exact story, article, or TED Talk to fit a unit I am doing, but I also feel the constant pressure to stay current while utilizing the latest and greatest tech and digital media, and I am sure I am not alone.

As a human being, I can see the societal value in shared experience, and as an educator, I believe it is crucial to create shared experiences where and when we can. Perhaps I am more concerned about this because I am a trained English teacher, and I feel that I am witnessing and experiencing the death of allusion. It is becoming far too common to reference classic stories, fables, or even something in pop culture, only to be met with blank stares of bewilderment. The importance of reading the same stories to learn and understand similar moral values and societal norms cannot be overstated. It doesn't have to be textbooks, and it doesn't have to be Shakespeare, although I think The Bard's works can provide some interesting and timely insights into the themes of power, fate, and free will. I fear that relying exclusively on the online world for resources may eventually leave us all reading "a tale told by an idiot, full of sound and fury, signifying nothing" (Shakespeare, *Macbeth*).

PAUSE FOR THOUGHT

1. Reflect on the shared experiences you had as a student, be it a class text, group project, production, or publication.
2. What can shared experiences provide individuals?
3. How can shared experiences provide opportunities for rich discussions with diverse perspectives?
4. How can we, as educators, ensure that our students will still have wide-ranging, meaningful shared experiences?
5. How do you and your colleagues create shared experiences within your departments or schools?

EDUCATIONAL ANECDOTE: THE POWER OF POETRY IN THE DIGITAL AGE

Contributed by **Marie Metaphor Specht**,
2023 Victoria Poet Laureate and Educator

Over the course of my teaching career, I have repeatedly seen the profound impact of exposing learners to poetry and spoken word. I have witnessed young people find their voice in poetry and become empowered to speak their truth, accessing both the power of language and the power of being seen in their complex humanity. Oral storytelling is one of our oldest human traditions. There are many examples of moving poetry performances to be found online, but to really experience the magic of spoken word, we need to engage with it live and in person. There is a unique kind of focused energy in the room when a youth shares their poem in a workshop or performance space. By its nature, spoken word is inherently vulnerable. The truths youth explore in their poetry are often a passionate reflection of how they see the world. Those who explore this form quickly realise that the most compelling spoken-word poems draw from the poet's lived experience to engage with bigger themes of what it is to be human here and now. Yes, it can be high stakes to be vulnerable in this way, but the rewards are substantial.

The spoken-word community is known for acceptance and celebration. There is a palpable, electric feeling of connection in these classrooms, cafes, and theatres full of young people sharing their poetry out loud and in person. These poets have tapped into the incredible power that comes with telling your own story in a way that others will not only hear it but also celebrate it. This is especially true for individuals from underrepresented or marginalized groups and individuals who have faced struggles in their lives. Many youth poets have taken a huge personal risk to share their vulnerable work on stage only to have it met with riotous cheers and applause. Spoken-word audiences tend to be effusively vocal in their recognition of moving poetry, risk-taking, and vulnerability. These students are not only being applauded for their grasp on language and their strong performance; they are being celebrated for who they are and how they see the world, for alchemizing their lived experience into art. It's the kind of art that reaches out and connects to other humans. The experience of being seen and celebrated in this way can truly change lives, and it is not something that can be found online.

One of the more profound examples of this happened when I started weekly poetry sessions at an alternative school for youth who are pregnant or parenting and young women and trans youth who have resisted conventional programs. Much of this resistance to conventional programs stems from adverse home conditions, trauma, addiction, and mental health issues. Most students at this school have transferred there after experiencing difficulties at other schools in our community. In this safe environment, a group of these learners started experiencing success in writing poetry and spoken word about their varied lived experiences. The success came from writing together and sharing their work face to face with the other participating students. This is not an easy thing to do for students who have been told repeatedly that they are not good at school.

In these weekly sessions, the poets became a close-knit group as they encouraged one another. We were able to celebrate their poetic successes and use them to build confidence among these learners which, incredibly, led to putting together a team for Victorious Voices, the local high school spoken-word festival. This was a huge win considering many of these students had a history of struggling to engage in school at all, let alone participate in a literary competition outside of school hours. In general, this school does not have teams of any kind that participate in events with other schools, and there was concern about how our learners would be welcomed: How would the students from regular public schools respond to poetry about being pregnant at fifteen, raising a child while finishing high school, or living on their own because their parent is incarcerated? How would they respond to these truths spoken by students who may have been their classmates before their circumstances changed?

It turns out these young poets were not only welcomed but celebrated. Witnessing those students speak their truth on stage, in front of their peers, was a highlight of my teaching career. The fact that they ended up placing third in the competition was just icing on the cake. Those moments onstage, being seen and applauded for their poetic accounts of their lived experiences, were pivotal for these young people. They created a window into a world where they can alchemize their struggles into art that is valued by their community.

As students move into young adulthood, memories of high school self-actualization can become touchstones of achievement and self-worth, reminders of who they are and the power of self-expression. This is a real, intrinsic validation that is impossible to get from a screen.

What is it about poetry and spoken word that can be so motivating for young people? Why do they get up on stage to speak their truths, even though it is a risk to be that vulnerable? A lot of it has to do with the supportive communities that are formed when we share creative work that is personal and important to us. This kind of sharing closes the spaces between people and allows us to connect and understand each other, fostering safer spaces. This sharing starts in classrooms or in small groups, then expands when these youth share their work in performance with other poets.

Here's what Neko Smart, (Victoria's 8th Youth Poet Laureate), has to say about poetry:

> "To say poetry has altered my life's trajectory would be an understatement. I would not be the person I am today had I not made the decision at sixteen years old to create my high school's first slam poetry team, to chase an idea into a passion. I have grappled with mental illness my whole life. Poetry as a means of creative expression allows me to process the world through the lens of my anxiety disorder. Through the craft, I have cultivated the most important connections in my life, been held by my community, and fostered necessary self-compassion. I truly believe in poetry's profound ability to enrich and sometimes even save young lives."

Marie Metaphor Specht is an educator, multidisciplinary artist, and poet living on the traditional territories of the Lək̓ʷəŋən and SENĆOŦEN speaking peoples. Marie has been coaching and mentoring youth poets for over a decade. She performs at a wide variety of venues ranging from interdisciplinary arts events to poetry slams and has been published in journals both in print and online. She believes in the power of stories shared.

Marie is the 2023 Poet Laureate of Victoria, BC, and her book, *Soft Shelters*, was released with Write Bloody North in the fall of 2023.

Author's note: I asked Marie to share her experiences with teaching spoken word poetry because I have noticed a disturbing trend of students sitting alone. Even when students are seated together in groups, they are often on their phones and silent. It is no wonder there has been a rise in youth feeling lonely and isolated. There is danger in isolation, for the individual and for society. Marie's experiences of working with youth through spoken word are a reminder of how important it is to encourage our students to engage in real-life, person-to-person activities. Clubs, groups, and teams have never been as important in our schools as they are now. In my opinion, they should not be optional. Participation in a club, group, team, or social activity in every year of school should be a requirement for graduation.

PAUSE FOR THOUGHT

1. What club, group, or team activities were you involved in when you were a student? How did those experiences and interactions impact you?
2. How does your school encourage students to get involved in clubs, groups, or teams?

CHAPTER 9

GETTING BACK TO GROUP WORK

Way back in 2016, an article in the *Harvard Business Review* noted that "collaboration is taking over the workplace." Indeed, that skill has only become more important as technology has continued to advance. A 2024 *Forbes* article highlighted the value of multi-generational collaboration, commenting that "when boomers share their experience and leadership, and Gen Z brings its digital fluency and innovative spirit to the table, the possibilities for groundbreaking solutions and organizational success become limitless." It is no surprise that one of the nine Key Essential Skills for the workplace, as identified by the Canadian government, is "Working with Others."

In answer to this call for collaboration in the marketplace, the skill has been identified as a core learning competency within education curricula in many schools worldwide, including many provinces of Canada. Buzzwords, such as *group-based learning, project-based learning*, and *collaborative learning,* are meant to inspire teachers at all levels to apply more group work opportunities for students in their classes. We hear a lot about collaboration, but many teachers struggle to implement strategies that effectively help their students understand and master the Collaboration Competency. I am one of those teachers. Many factors contribute to the challenge of teaching our students this essential life skill, but following the theme of this book, I believe one of the main culprits is sitting in the palm of a student's hand.

Years of coaching sports have given me valuable experiences that help me navigate the challenges in the classroom as a high school teacher. Believing that the long-term value of teamwork skills will help many of my students in their future career paths, I readily buy into the idea of collaborative learning in the classroom. I enthusiastically and thoughtfully set up group-based learning projects to harness the strengths of each individual student in a supportive and collaborative environment. At the very mention of the phrase *group project*, however, I am met with dejected huffs and eyerolls. Before I have time to describe the parameters of the assignment, multiple hands shoot into the air, followed by inquiries about whether students will be able to select the groups themselves. Even after I've gotten the class sorted in groups and working on their projects, students trickle to my desk, asking if they can switch groups, wondering if I am aware that so-and-so is not pulling their weight, and, voicing the top concern of many students, inquiring whether everyone in the group will be receiving the same grade. What I thought would be a week of students learning and collaborating leaves me dejected, tired, and confused. *Why, yet again, has a project that should have been fun and engaging taken such a negative turn?*

Aversion to group work did not initiate with the arrival of smartphones, nor is it an attitude exclusive to students. I have gone to many a professional-development event where the mere mention of breaking into groups from a speaker is immediately followed by a low grumble of annoyance from the audience. I admit that, wanting to sit and sip my morning coffee in peace, I am sometimes among the grumblers.

At a recent professional development event I attended, a session with *collaboration* in the title, the speaker had organized a series of activities involving group work. When it became evident that no one wanted to get up from their chairs, the speaker said something along the lines of high school teachers being the worst sell for these kinds of activities. She had no problem motivating elementary and middle school teachers to get up and collaborate, but when it came to high school teachers, like our own audience, we couldn't be bothered to move and were more content to brainstorm with someone sitting right beside us.

I do not believe that smartphones are the sole culprit contributing to this aversion to group work at the high school level. The pressure and competitive culture of achieving high grades and concerns about freeloading peers certainly play a role. Phones, however, have played a significant role in the underdevelopment of students' social skills, which they will need if they are going to learn to collaborate effectively in the workplace. These clear deficits in their abilities—and the risk posed to their future success as a result—make it more important than ever that we guide them in developing these skills via well-intentioned group work activities.

Patrick Lencioni, a well-known teamwork and organizational health consultant, writes about the importance of teamwork skills in his book The *Five Dysfunctions of Team*. He states, "Not finance. Not strategy. Not technology. It is teamwork that remains the ultimate competitive advantage, both because it is so powerful and so rare." The stay-at-home mandates during the Covid lockdowns sparked an increasing push towards remote work. Some may argue that society is evolving to work in an online world, making working socially (in person) with others a less-vital skill set. I disagree, and so do some of the biggest tech companies in the world.

While it is easy to envision a computer programmer and other tech industry employees diligently working in front of computers nestled inside their individual cubicles, many companies in Silicon Valley encourage their engineers to "work together, in part because studies show that groups tend to innovate faster, see mistakes more quickly, and find better solutions to problems." In many ways, the increasing emphasis on teamwork skills can be attributed to advances in technology and the creation of a world where information is readily available for anyone who wants to find it. Roles in the workplace used to be much more defined, with employees being hired based on previous education, training, and skills; however, a study titled *Teamwork in Modern Organizations: Implications for Technology Education* noted that, "today, information is becoming available to everyone to an equal extent" and "young employees in the workplace . . . are frequently more in command of communication technologies and access to information than are their superiors." This mirrors a shift in the classroom where "the teacher is no longer the only source of knowledge" and instead must "become a facilitator of the learning process."

A teacher's role in the classroom has evolved from lecturing at the front of the room and imparting knowledge to facilitating the learning process and developing learning competencies within their students. Like the Nine Essential Skills of the Canadian government (Numeracy, Oral Communication, Working with Others, Continuous Learning, Reading Text, Writing, Thinking, Document Use, Digital Skills), curricular competencies of many education ministries are much broader, focusing on skill development over specific content delivery. This focus is meant to help students better adapt to an ever-evolving workplace where they will need to work with others in order to "solve issues that are more and more complex and multidisciplinary."

Humans are social creatures. It is why we have evolved. The iGen may be on their phones and staring at screens more than any other generation and age group, but I am not so sure they want to be. Among the many reasons that the lockdowns and online learning were a disaster for so many is the reality that we crave human contact, not screentime. This craving is also the reason why students are addicted to social media; in a roundabout way, they are searching for social contact with others and finding it in the form of pictures, texts, and videos.

LESSENING ANXIETY ABOUT WORKING WITH OTHERS

We know that collaboration is an essential skill. We also know group work offers benefits to the collective and the individual in terms of social interaction, connection, and the general advancement of society. So how do we convince our students that the next group project isn't the end of life as they know it? (Okay, maybe that seems overly dramatic, but then so are those eyerolls.)

The answer, at least in part, is to go back to the *why*! If students understand the benefits and opportunities of working with, learning from, and harnessing the skills of others, they will be far more likely to approach group work with a positive mindset.

Collaborative work exists everywhere, from the family nucleus, places of work, personal friend groups, online gaming, and neighbourhood communities. Anytime we are working on a common goal with others, we are doing group work. To lessen anxiety about working with others, begin by reminding students that they already have experience with group work, even if they don't recognize it as such. Randall Hansen, author of the "Benefits and Problems With Student Teams," emphasizes that teachers can enhance the importance and value of learning teamwork, by helping students to understand that "the ability to work in teams and to lead teams" is not just something they need for everyday life; it "has become an important skill to master and one that employers" are actively seeking.

Once you've established the why—the purpose and value—of group work, you can further lessen students' anxiety by addressing their most common questions and concerns. When students are presented with a group-work activity, the same questions are often raised. Lessening anxiety about working with others requires a mindset shift from anxiety mindset to teamwork mindset.

When presented with group work, the Anxiety Mindset asks the following questions:

- How will these groups be decided?
- Whom am I going to be working with?
- What will I have to do?
- Why are we doing this?
- How will this assignment be graded?

When presented with group work, the Teamwork Mindset asks the following questions:

- What skills will others bring to the group?
- Whom am I going to be learning from, and whom will I be teaching?
- What skills am I bringing to help with group success?
- What am I going to learn about myself?
- What new concepts or ideas will this assignment teach me?

If we can shift student thinking and adjust their mindset when it comes to working with others, then assigning group work activities will be not only be easier, it will also be something students look forward to.

For a printable PDF poster, please visit my website heretolearn.ca or scan the QR code below.

GROUP WORK

ANXIETY MINDSET vs. TEAMWORK MINDSET

Anxiety Mindset	Teamwork Mindset
HOW WILL THESE GROUPS BE DECIDED?	WHICH SKILLS WILL OTHERS BRING TO THE GROUP?
WHOM AM I GOING TO BE WORKING WITH?	WHOM AM I GOING TO LEARN FROM AND WHOM WILL I BE TEACHING?
WHAT WILL I HAVE TO DO?	WHICH SKILLS AM I BRINGING TO HELP WITH GROUP SUCCESS?
WHY ARE WE DOING THIS?	WHAT AM I GOING TO LEARN ABOUT MYSELF?
HOW WILL THIS ASSIGNMENT BE GRADED?	WHICH NEW CONCEPTS OR IDEAS WILL THIS ASSIGNMENT TEACH ME?

Here to Learn

Partnerships that Work

I noted earlier that one of the first questions students ask when they hear the dreaded phrase *group project* is if they can choose their partners. Often, they will ask to work with their friends, using the excuse that they will work better together. Studies reveal, however, "that students are more likely to have a positive learning experience when groups are selected by the professor." Teacher-selected groups also provide more realistic preparation for the real-world workplace "in which supervisors place workers in teams rather than allowing them to self-select."

Allow adequate time to think through which students should be grouped together and how many should be in each group. In my experience, three is the magic number for most groups, but the total can vary depending on the size and complexity of the project. Remind your students that the process mirrors the real world in which employers will have them working with others whose skill sets are different from their own. Encourage them to embrace the reality of these differences, recognize the opportunity they have to learn from others, and discover more about themselves and the skill sets they will need to develop to better function in collaborative environments.

Defining the Roles

Students need to understand that working with others is not a deterrent to their individual success but rather an opportunity for growth and learning that can contribute to a much more successful outcome with their final project. Examining how Pixar fosters collective creativity, the company's co-founder Ed Catmull explains that Pixar creators reinforce "the mindset that we're all learning, and it's fun to learn together." He believes that the best projects are produced when "everyone is fully invested in helping everyone else turn out the best work." Pixar employees understand that "people learn from and inspire each other," and while the collaborative process is messy, "it's far better to learn about problems from colleagues when there's still time to fix them than from the audience after it's too late." The same goes for students. Feedback from peers that can help to edit and refine a project before handing it to the teacher to be assessed should result in higher achievement.

As students begin to work on a group project, the first step should be to discuss their skill sets and areas of weakness to better understand what each individual student can contribute to the overall project as well as areas that will need guidance or support from others. This will require students to be a little vulnerable with one another, which is something that the teacher may need to facilitate during a guided activity. While this may be an uncomfortable step, it is important in fostering trust and positive collaborative skills. If students can gain an appreciation for others' needs and roles within the group, then their individualistic attitudes could shift to the collective. These open discussions could prompt group members to understand that to understand that students who might who might have formerly been perceived as freeloaders may not be trying to take advantage of others' efforts but are self-conscious about the value of their contributions to overall group performance. When students know what is expected of them, they are more confident in their abilities. Additionally, with clearly defined roles, their work tends to be more focused and efficient.

Finding the Common Goal

A study by Le, Ha, et al. on "Collaborative Learning Practices: Teacher and Student Perceived Obstacles to Effective Student Collaboration," found that "when [students] started to work in groups, they did not know how to collaborate effectively," and that their "lack of collaborative skills such as accepting opposing viewpoints, giving elaborate explanations, providing and receiving help, and negotiating prevented them working productively in groups." In the same study, "18 out of 19 teachers reported that their students predominantly did not know how to use collaborative skills effectively," commenting that their students "rarely share their opinions, while others defensively argue for their idea."

For teams to work effectively together, all members must understand that they are working towards a common goal. In a school setting, highlighting specific collaborative performance goals such as communication, providing and receiving critical feedback, and evidence of cooperation with the academic goals of the assigned project from the outset can be beneficial when attempting to convince students of the collaborative project's value. Including students in the goal-setting process will help students take ownership of the goals and recognize how their individual success coincides with the team's success. You might even choose to have groups set their own learning goals, focusing on collaborative tasks that can only be achieved by working with their team members.

Note that while a common goal can be achieving a high grade on the assignment, that cannot be the only goal. Common learning goals should include concepts, such as all students feeling like their efforts are well represented in the final product, engaging in progress check-ins to problem solve, and ensuring that pace and group members are on target for project completion.

Amy Edmondson, an organizational behavioural scientist and Harvard professor of leadership and organizational learning, believes that individuals who are "on the same page, with common goals and a shared appreciation for what they're up against," set the stage for psychological safety, a term she defines as "a belief that one will not be punished or humiliated for speaking up with ideas, questions, concerns, or mistakes." Setting common collaborative goals and creating a psychologically safe learning environment in a high school class setting is crucial when fostering trust and encouraging students to take risks while working with others.

STEPS FOR POSITIVE COLLABORATIVE GROUP WORK

1. Groups should be intentionally set by the teacher. This includes size and composition. (In my experience, three is the magic number.)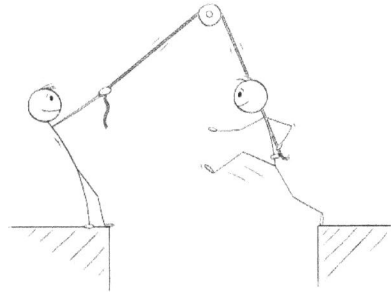
2. Students within the group should discuss their strengths and weaknesses in order to better define their roles and responsibilities within the group.
3. Groups should define their individual and common goals.
4. Students should reflect on their group work experience and the skill sets they enhanced while working with others, as well as further opportunities for growth.
5. Teachers should reiterate the skill sets built during the group work experience throughout the project. The final project should be *symbolic* of the learning and the competencies developed throughout the journey of its creation.

Smartphones and technology offer many interesting opportunities for collaborative experiences; however, most have been designed for users who are working at a distance from one another and with the assumption that users already have collaborative skill sets. It is not enough for teachers to assign group work activities and then cross their fingers in hopes that collaborative competencies will be fostered during the project. Collaboration needs to be intentionally built in and guided throughout the group work experience.

PAUSE FOR THOUGHT

1. Reflect on your group work experiences when you were a student. Were they positive or negative? What made them so?
2. How do you assign group work in your own classroom?
3. How do you assess work completed in groups in your classroom?
4. How are the activities you assign enhanced by making them group-based?
5. What are the skills and hidden curriculum that come from group work in school?
6. What changes can you make that would ensure purposeful group work in your classroom?

CHAPTER 10

EMBRACING THE TECH

The following is taken from an essay I wrote that was published in Vol. 62. No.1 of the *English Practice Journal*, 2022. It highlights the struggles and benefits of the teacher-controlled versus the co-designed classroom and exemplifies how advancing technology in our schools, although at times intimidating, when purposefully applied, can enhance the teaching and learning experience.

At the end of the 2016/17 school year, the head of my high school's English department, forced to "use it or lose it," spent the remainder of the department budget on twenty studio-quality microphones. There was a movement to use more technology and media elements in the classroom, and while there was not yet a plan to put them to use, the fancy silver-ball microphones, reminiscent of retro-radio studio programming days, seemed a better use of funds than adding yet another class set of *Hamlet* or *A Catcher in the Rye*. It was the sleepy last days of the school year when the June sun heats up the classroom to Hades-like conditions and a few lingering students can be spotted clearing out scrunched-up paper assignments from their lockers while teachers frantically tally final marks and input report card comments. Knowing I had the task of teaching three grade 12 English classes the next year and feeling personally challenged to do something worthy of the brand-new microphones I had volunteered to shelve, I began to brainstorm the beginnings of a class podcast project. I had been flirting with the idea of coming up with a project that could somehow use the power of story to connect the students with their community, and these microphones, which seemed to almost be challenging me to do something worthy of them, provided a shiny new tool I hoped would inspire and entice the students as much as the mics were enticing me.

We had just begun talks about the implementation of the new BC Curriculum—a concept-based, competency-driven curriculum modelled for education in the twenty-first century that "enables and supports increasingly personalized learning, through quality teaching and learning, flexibility and choice, and high standards." Early iterations of the new curriculum had shown a revamping of English at the high school level, allowing for student choice in specific areas: Literary Studies, Spoken Language, New Media, Composition, and Creative Writing. With a new focus on a learner-centred curriculum, an announcement had just been made that the next school year would be the last for the English 12 provincial. This announcement was met with a varying mix of relief and optimism from those who wanted to see a shift away from the postcolonial practices of terminology memorization but with concern and disapproval from those who believed in the comprehension, analysis, and writing merits of the standardized structure.

I am not sure what made me think I could take on a project of this magnitude. I had no training in the technical side of podcast development or any idea how I was going to structure it, but I found myself bored with teaching the same things and encouraged by the opportunities of the new curriculum. With little idea of the ride I or my students were in for, I approached my principal with my initial ideas and the rationale of how the project reflected the new curriculum. I was given an enthusiastic "go ahead" to set the train in motion for the next school year.

The inspiration for this project came because, like most teachers, I intuitively understood that my students needed and were craving something different from their learning and from me. I could feel the shift from that "sage on the stage" to the "guide on the side" occurring in real time. All teachers have a voice inside that lets them know when they are truly reaching their students and when they are not. It is what allows us to quickly pivot and refocus our efforts on something else. Listening to that voice gave me the courage to implement and follow through with the Podcast Project, which is why I now understand that in order to maximize the potential of individual students and their unique learning needs, co-designed and student-centred learning should be a main focus of curriculum development . . . but at the time, it was all just a feeling and theory.

To fully commit to what I was calling the Podcast Project, I knew I was going to have to ignore some of the teacher training that had been drilled into me and let go of the safety in the routine that I had gotten so used to. I now recognize that I was slowly becoming one of the "casualties of the knowledge society," often looking to acquire standardized and proven instructional strategies that had already been preordained by others, "without contemplating the effects upon the students as distinctive cultural and emotional beings." I am a product of teacher-centred instruction and have been trained to teach in that style. Promoted by educational and developmental psychology legends John Dewey and Lev Vygotsky, the concept of the constructivist method "states that students learn more by doing and experiencing rather than by observing." I completely understand that. But, like others, it was taking me time to get used to this shift towards student-centred instruction where "the teacher shares control of the classroom, and students are allowed to explore, experiment, and discover on their own."

Not letting my discomfort with the unknown deter me, I outlined the initial goals of the project: (1) to connect people and the community through story, (2) to help students develop skills they could use beyond the classroom, (3) to work collaboratively as a whole class, and perhaps the most ambitious,

(4) to have a completed and published podcast series by the end of the school year. I had no idea if these were necessarily S.M.A. R. T. (Specific, Measurable, Achievable, Realistic, Time-Bound) goals, but I wasn't going to let the unknowns hold me back from trying. The previous few years of teaching had revealed a very real and growing fear of failure in many of my students, and while I preached to not let the fear of failure hold them back, and that valuable learning can occur through failure, I knew that to ultimately show them how to challenge it, I had to model challenging my own fear of failing with the project. From the outset, I assured the students that no matter what happened, a lot of learning would occur, and they would only be graded on what we managed to accomplish over the course of the year. I reiterated the "we" to let them know that I was fully relinquishing my place on the stage to join them on this learning journey.

Despite assurances, the initial reception to the presentation of this project was mixed. Most of the students had never done a project that required the commitment of the entire school year, and many were hesitant about doing something that had never been attempted before by a teacher who did not have all the answers. One of the main areas of concern voiced by the students was the worry that this project would take away valuable time needed to prepare them for the heavily weighted (40 percent) English provincial. According to the 2016 Canadian Census, Oak Bay, the region my high school is situated in, contains one of the most highly educated populations in the world, with 59 percent holding a university certificate, diploma, or degree at bachelor level or above. That is 30 percent higher than the national average. Not only is education highly valued at Oak Bay, but a certain kind of education, one that prepares the students for the academic world of post-secondary institutions, is expected. To secure buy-in, I literally made a promise to the students that they would have adequate time to prepare for the provincial . . . which was nine months away.

In a linear school, we have three fifty-minute classes each week. Once the initial phase of introducing the project was complete, one day a week, chosen by the students, was dedicated to working on the podcast exclusively. The other two days were dedicated to covering course content, which included a novel study and units dedicated to poetry, creative writing, and short story. Sticking to some of the traditional content and methods of learning and teaching provided some reassurance and balance to students, parents, and me. I wanted to go off the beaten path, to truly dive into twenty-first-century educational practices, which, according to Frans Meijers, teach that an "absence of dialogue and the subsequent lack of control by students over their own learning processes [can result] in students' lack of intrinsic motivation with regards to their studies." However, I was wary that the students, used to a certain style of learning, would only follow me so far.

This project had the potential to check off all of the Core Competencies included in the new curriculum: Communication, Creative and Critical Thinking, Personal Awareness and Responsibility, Positive Personal and Cultural Identity, and Social Awareness and Responsibility; things important to educational professionals but that rarely matter to students. For this project to have any chance of succeeding, it required the students to care, to fully engage, and for that, they needed the opportunity to do something they were interested in and to have it mean something. Student-centred learning treats the students "as co-creators within the learning process and as individuals with relevant ideas about how learning takes place." However, I also wanted to make this bigger than them, to hold them accountable, and to see what this extra element would produce. With a vague idea how, I ambitiously told them that whatever we created would be published and available to the public through a major podcasting platform. This meant that the students would be officially credited and that any skills and experiences worked on during the process could be added to applications and future resumes. For the students, the potential to engage with the real world and boost their university applications was the final motivation needed. I had them hooked.

The project was divided into three sections: pre-production, production, and post-production. Pre-production was focused on introducing the project, deciding on topics, assigning roles and groups, and goal setting.

With a theme of connecting community through story, the classes voted on the areas they wanted to focus on. I had pre-selected three: the homeless community, the senior community, and the school community itself. Conveniently, each class united in selecting a specific and unique direction. Having gotten to know my students and their personalities, I was not surprised by which focus each class chose. Very shortly after selecting, each of the classes, through a class vote, came up with a unique series title: "*Stories from the Street*, *Through the Years*, and *This Teen Life*," all existing under the umbrella of the Podcast Project. While difficult to manage, the benefit of having each class take ownership over their own unique series created a sense of responsibility and healthy competition, which seemed to harness their focus.

The next step was assigning roles. Taking every opportunity to develop real-world skills, I tasked the students with applying, via a formal pitch-styled cover letter, for the area and position they wanted to work in.

1. Story/Creative
   a. Interviewer
   b. Story designer/editor
   c. Talent—voice of the podcast
2. Technical/Production
   a. Producer—team oversight and general manager
   b. Technician—sound, editing, publishing
3. Creative Design/Marketing
   a. Creative Design—visuals, music theme
   b. Marketing and advertising

With their pitch, the students needed to include research and information about their chosen area, clearly demonstrating their understanding of what would be required of them. In 2013, a team of researchers that included Meijers and Annemie Winters, wrote an article in the *Journal of Constructivist Psychology* that claimed, "educational culture is monological and focused on control by means of tests . . . most teachers are uncertain about their abilities to help students in developing a career narrative." Helping the students to define a career path was not my goal, but I hoped that giving them the opportunity to work in different and chosen areas would give them a small taste of the vast and diverse opportunities available to them. Once selected and divided into teams, each group began the brainstorming and goal-setting process.

Student-centred learning means that the teacher must let go of the "teacher" role, becoming a coach or instigator, there to assist as the students explore and teach themselves but never give away answers. In some ways, it was easy to let go of the teacher role because I didn't have the answers to give, but I found that one of the most difficult components of this project was navigating student participation and effort. With each group taking on different tasks, some being reliant on the work of others, the workload was often imbalanced, requiring students to help in different areas of the project when it was needed or when they found themselves with little to do. Adding to this, each of the classes worked at a very different pace from the others, with one jumping into action from the beginning and others needing more time for preparation. From the outset, I felt that I had bitten off far more than I could chew. We had set some lofty goals with little idea of how they would be accomplished. Not knowing how, while initially anxiety-inducing for students so used to being told exactly what they needed to do in order to get the grade they desired, forced them off a narrow path and gave them the permission to explore the unknown. Letting go of traditional teaching methods was new territory for me too. It felt like taking my hands off of the steering wheel, and it did not take long for the momentum of the project to propel me and the students in unforeseen directions.

There is a famous, overused, and often misquoted line from the film *Field of Dreams* that, "If you build it, [they] will come." Perhaps, what is more accurate to say is that if you have good intentions, people will feel inspired to help. At least, this is how it went for the Podcast Project. An initial district grant of $500 offered the project the funds to get started, but once the students began inquiring, we were gifted platforms for editing (TwistedWave), offered access to interviews, including an exclusive with the Mayor of Victoria, and given local media coverage. I had intended to give the students one day a week to work on the project in class, but without prompting, they began working on this project on their own time.

Evan*, a student diagnosed with ADHD who struggled in the traditional classroom, found his stride with the variety of work that this project offered. He connected with Rev. Al Tysick, a man who has received countless awards for his volunteer work with the Victoria homeless community, joining him for 5 a.m. rides, to both interview and fully experience what and who Tysick deals with on a daily basis. Evan's efforts resulted in three twenty-minute episodes, which connected him and others to an often-overlooked part of our society. I wanted students to connect to their community through story. What I didn't realise at the time was that I was applying place-based pedagogy which, as a response to "standardized pedagogy that neglects local human and ecological communities," draws on progressive traditions of multidisciplinary, authentic learning in order to extend education beyond the walls of the school.

In Evan's own words, his experience made him realise that just talking to members of the homeless community "means the world to a lot of them. It's not something that should just always be a thing. It's just not something I think is acceptable in a country that is so beloved."**

Other episodes that emerged from *Stories from the Street* focused on individual stories gathered during interviews at a local homeless shelter a mere fifteen-minute drive from the parking lot of Oak Bay but a world away for many of the students.

Mariah, another student working on interviews for *Stories from the Street*, commented in a final reflection that for her the firsthand experience "made homelessness the monster and not the actual homeless population, as is often done in the media." It was the exposure to these members of society that prompted Mariah and others to reach out for an interview with the city Mayor Lisa Helps.

---

* Student Names have been changed.
**Student quotations were collected from the reflection of their learning journey using the Core and Curricular Competencies.

While I accompanied the students to the meeting at City Hall, I did not participate in setting up the completely student-driven interview. Not only would that prove to be a lesson in dealing with public authority figures, it demonstrated the ongoing and frustrating political struggles behind the issue.

Place-based education seeks to connect learning to real-world experiences, where "students can construct meaningful connections among cultural, political, and social issues." The opportunity was certainly giving the students an experience that no textbook could provide. From Maria's point of view, "Helps talked about how they (the city) were working to provide affordable housing, while the people at the shelter were talking about how it's usually the homeless that help the homeless and how they are the ones looking out for each other."

During the editing process, a few of the students came to me, conflicted about including sections of the interview with Lisa Helps that contradicted research and information gathered from interviews with the homeless. They were concerned that including parts of the interview would reflect badly on the mayor. This completely unintended obstacle provided a valuable opportunity for me to reinforce the importance of the students trusting their process and perspective as gained through their research and experiences. Ultimately, the authorship was theirs. Where a typical class lesson may have had the students reading and examining an article in order to "identify bias, contradictions, distortions, and omissions," this project was providing a real-life experiential lesson (B. C. English 12 Curriculum).

Similar learning outcomes were seen in the other two groups. The *Through the Years* team reached out to local care homes and senior community centres looking for stories and lessons that senior citizens in the community wanted to share with graduating senior students.

After conducting interviews with two senior citizens, both of whom shared their personal stories of immigrating to Canada at a young age, Nicole, one of my students, reflected that "listening to how important their family background and heritage is to them made me think about my heritage and where I come from. After this project, I now see the importance of knowing where I come from and being able to discuss my heritage with my parents and grandparents."

Kiera, another one of my students, created such an impactful bond with her elderly interviewee Carmen, that Carmen ended up attending Kiera's graduation.

Those working on *This Teen Life* took on topics ranging from the difficulties of fitting in, which included an interview with a teenage Syrian refugee, to gun control and lockdown drills, and issues that students living in the LGBTQ community face.

About halfway into the school year, still unsure of whether or not we were going to be able to produce a viable podcast, I felt reassured by all of the lessons and skills the students were learning and the impact it was having on them.

During the winter months, again unprompted by me, the class working on *Stories from the Street* started a school sock-and-blanket drive and convinced the grad class to donate $300 towards gift cards for the homeless. Not to be outdone, the class working on *Through the Years* started a Christmas-card campaign, creating cards with messages from the graduating seniors to be given to those living in care homes who may be feeling lonely or depressed at that time of the year.

Although we were feeling fairly smug about what the project had already accomplished, the reality of the work involved in the post-production phase and the steepness of the learning curve abruptly knocked the wind from our sails. My technological ignorance became painfully evident and demanded that the students take the lead to a noticeable degree, switching the power balance in the classroom.

The post-production phase included splicing the episodes together with voice recording, music, and sound effects; eventually uploading to a podcasting platform; and marketing and design. It required a huge amount of effort, patience, and research.

I share some of the concerns from those who worry that with student-centred approaches, teachers "are being pushed to go deep without equipping students with the breadth of background knowledge needed to succeed." The experience forced me to trust the process and the resourcefulness of my students. Teaching each other what we knew and were learning as we went, each class and I began piecing together a final product. Those starting to wonder if the Podcast Project would actually come to fruition were given renewed faith when, on May 8th, they heard the first four-minute preview episode of *Through the Years*. Six more episodes were published on May 22nd, and by the time the last microphone was shelved, the Podcast Project had yielded seventeen episodes, all available for public access through major podcasting platforms.

One of the last and crucial pieces to the Podcast Project puzzle was the assessment. With the implementation of the new curriculum, the BC Ministry of Education has stood behind the idea that "curriculum should drive evaluation or assessment, and assessment should not drive curriculum." However, concern has been expressed that the "lack of alignment between curriculum and assessment," combined with a lack of information, has resulted in an increased workload for many teachers. I knew going into our project that assessment would be difficult, but with the belief that curriculum should drive assessment and not the other way around, I did not want the potential difficulties or workload of assessing the project to get in the way or lessen the value of what could be learned.

I had been keeping track of the process and knew who had stepped up more than others, but providing a fair and balanced assessment was not something I could do alone. The Communication competency of the BC Curriculum "enables the student to become an active part in the assessment process so as to exchange information, experiences, and ideas, to explore the world around them." Drawing on the freedom in assessment that this competency allows, and wanting the students to acknowledge what they had learned during the project, I tasked them with writing a mark defence that included reporting on a selection of the Core and Curricular Competencies. The reflection and mark they assigned themselves heavily influenced their final project grade and turned out to be one of the most meaningful learning moments (at least for me) of the entire project. In my experience, especially at this academically focused high school, "grading and ranking is often grounded on norm-based criteria that lead to harmful competition among learners, which weighs down on true learning for all and genuine collaborative learning."

At some point, I am not sure exactly when, the students stopped asking me about how the project was going to be graded and started focusing solely on the final product. As a final exclamation point highlighting what this project meant to the students, the very last episode, a six-minute piece reflecting on the students' experience during the project, was sent to me a week after the school had closed its doors and report cards had been handed out. The students were technically free. There were no grades on the line or pressure to add anything else. They simply wanted to see the episode complete and uploaded.

Teachers should follow their intuition and do what they feel is right for their teaching style and their students' learning needs. I went into the Podcast Project with the confidence of a seasoned teacher, ready to adapt or yield where necessary. The students involved were in grade 12, already equipped with background knowledge and many of the skills needed for the project. I believe student-centred practices should be given proper scaffolding and attention to learning outcomes; however, I write this with the intention of encouraging others, especially those with hesitations about student-centred education, to not let the confines of teacher-centred practices or anxiety about unknown challenges get in the way of attempting something that could lead to valuable outcomes for the students. While there are things I would change if given the opportunity to do this project again, I can confidently report that the skills attained, relationships fostered, and memorable learning journey the project afforded will undoubtedly have a longer-lasting impact than any score achieved on a standardized test.

PODCASTING IN YOUR CLASS

Podcasts are a literacy tool (often free) you can use, and you do not have to take on a whole podcast project or get students to make a podcast to see the benefits in your classroom. Listening to a podcast in class, as a whole class, engages  students in a shared experience while allowing them the opportunity to imagine the story or scenario for themselves. In classrooms with diverse learners and a range of literacy levels, listening to podcasts can mimic the benefits of a shared reading experience while minimizing some of the accessibility barriers. For learners who require additional exposure to the text, podcasts can be accessed multiple times and played at a speed that suits the learners' needs. Student engagement increases when learners are prompted to engage in active listening rather than passive listening by taking notes or completing worksheets to follow along with the podcast content.

10 Practical Benefits of Podcasts

Accessibility. Available on many platforms and devices, podcasts can be accessed easily. Students who miss listening in class can access content on their own devices and on their own time.

1. **Cost.** They are often free.
2. **Variety.** With more than five million podcasts covering thousands of topics, you can find a podcast that addresses almost any content you can think of.
3. **Whole-class participation.** Listening together keeps the class on the same page.
4. **Skill development.** Students practice their listening and comprehension skills.

5. **Vocabulary.** Listening to the spoken word enhances language acquisition for second-language learners and expands the vocabulary of those listening in their native language.
6. **Shared experience.** Listening together gives us a common activity that we can discuss later.
7. **Imagination.** Mentally picturing the scenes and stories engages the imagination in a way that seeing graphical representations does not.
8. **Authentic voices.** Podcasts allow individuals to share their stories and personal perspectives.
9. **Manageability.** With a finite start and end point, podcasts can seem less intimidating than traditional texts.

PAUSE FOR THOUGHT

1. How do you incorporate podcasts in your classroom?
2. In which ways can podcasts or podcasting platforms be utilized in your classroom?
3. What is your approach regarding new and innovative technology and its use in your classroom?

CHAPTER 11

THE DIGITAL CLASSROOM
(ACKNOWLEDGING THE *DIGITALEPHANT* IN THE CLASSROOM)

No matter what advances technology makes in the field of education, I believe that neither teacher-guided instruction nor teachers themselves have or ever will become obsolete. Students may be able to look up endless information, pictures, and videos about climbing a mountain, and they are even able to have generative AI tools write a narrative about the climb, but (as mentioned using the mountain metaphor before) the journey will be far more fulfilling if they climb it themselves and far safer with a guide at their side.

When students embark on a journey (learning or otherwise), it is the guide who makes sure everyone packs what they need. The guide even keeps a few backups on hand (water tabs, fully stocked first-aid kit) in case someone forgets to bring an essential supply. The guide has taken the route and knows the destination—and that there are many paths to get there. She knows which paths are the most direct, which ones have the best views, and which ones are going to take longer or be more challenging. She takes her group and their abilities and interests into account as she plans the route, and she may even ask for their input. Are they up for a challenge? Do they want to see waterfalls? Are they exhausted because it stormed last night and their tent flooded, and today they just need to take it easy?

The teacher knows the strengths and weakness and supplies of each member in the group (student conferences, portfolios, and diagnostic assessments). Because of that, she can be confident that some students can handle heading off on an excursion and still be able to meet the group at the summit or back at base camp (group inquiry projects). Others will need her help every step of the way. She periodically reminds them to put their phones away so they can 1) enjoy the views and 2) avoid falling off a cliff because they're watching a cat video or reading a friend's post and not paying attention to where they're walking. Occasionally, though, she asks them to pull out their phones to determine whether a plant or bug is dangerous, take photos to document the journey, or learn how to use the compass app.

Along this journey, there may be points at which the guide learns something from those she's leading. Someone who has a fascination with a particular plant, animal, or insect may be able to teach the whole group something new. And there may be points when they all have to work together to figure out a new or unexpected challenge—like how to cross the river when the bridge has been washed out or how to make dinner when the butane tank runs out of fuel. In those moments, the teacher is right there in the middle of things, working and learning with her students.

The Ever-Evolving Student

While the advances in technology—including YouTube, the internet, and social media—have changed not only how our students learn but our students themselves, they have not changed the importance of having a teacher, mentor, and guide along the learning journey. The dramatic changes that have occurred in a very short period demand that we, as educators, make some changes as well.

Patience levels and the ability to maintain sustained attention have become far more limited. The rate at which we receive information, the number of images we see in a day, and the constant desire to check our phones have made everyone more distractible and easier to pull off task. Having information so readily available in the palm of our hands has impacted our ability to memorize information, and for many students, has made them question why they need to know or be able to do certain things that their phones can do for them. Social etiquettes, such as maintaining eye contact and sustaining focus on a particular person or activity, have all but disappeared.

Students see their phones and technology as learning tools, and many teachers see them as learning distractions. Regardless of whether phones are banned from the learning environment, their impacts will still be felt. If we do not find a middle ground, the classroom will increasingly become a frustrating space for all. Difficult as it may be, as adults and as professional educators, it is our responsibility to adjust to how students learn in the tech-advanced classroom and to teach our students responsible habits that will help them socially function in a world outside our walls.

NAVIGATING CHATGPT AND OTHER AI CHATBOTS

The weekend I learned about ChatGPT, I stayed in bed, drinking coffee and playing with the technology. I wanted to understand exactly what it was about. Its capabilities blew me away. I sat in wonder while it dished out answer after answer to the questions and thematic stems I had typed in the message bar. My wife, also an English teacher, sat beside me. As we spent the morning reading five-paragraph essays that were being written in seconds before our eyes, and quite often better than many of our students could currently write, we turned to each other and acknowledged how this technological advancement was going to change education, society, and the working world as we knew it.

WHO BETTER TO ASK ABOUT AI THAN CHATGPT?

ChatGPT and similar AI technologies have the potential to impact education in several ways:

- **Access to Information:** ChatGPT can provide students with instant access to a vast amount of information on a wide range of topics. It can assist in research, help answer questions, and offer insights that might otherwise be time-consuming or challenging to find. This can expand educational opportunities, especially for students in underserved areas or with limited resources.
- **Personalized Learning:** ChatGPT can support personalized learning experiences by adapting to individual student needs. It can provide tailored explanations, offer additional examples, or suggest resources based on a student's specific inquiries or learning preferences. This individualized feedback can enhance student engagement and promote self-directed learning.
- **Writing Assistance:** ChatGPT can act as a writing aid, helping students improve their writing skills by offering suggestions, providing alternative phrasing, or assisting with grammar and syntax. It can offer constructive feedback and contribute to the development of students' writing abilities.
- **Critical Thinking and Digital Literacy:** The use of ChatGPT in classrooms can promote critical thinking and digital literacy skills. Students can learn to analyze and evaluate AI-generated content, discern reliable information from potentially biased or inaccurate responses, and develop a deeper understanding of the strengths and limitations of AI technology.

- **Collaboration and Communication:** ChatGPT can facilitate collaboration and communication among students. It can be used as a tool for brainstorming, idea generation, and peer feedback. Students can engage in conversational exchanges with ChatGPT, encouraging dialogue and exploration of different perspectives.
- **Ethical Considerations:** The integration of ChatGPT in education provides an opportunity to discuss ethical considerations surrounding AI technology. Students can explore topics such as privacy, bias, responsible AI use, and the impact of AI on society. These discussions foster critical thinking, digital citizenship, and ethical decision-making.
- **Future Skills Development:** As AI becomes increasingly prevalent, understanding and utilizing AI tools like ChatGPT can be valuable for students' future careers. Familiarity with AI technologies and their applications can equip students with relevant skills in fields such as data analysis, natural language processing, and human–AI collaboration.

It is important to note that while ChatGPT can provide valuable support, it is not a substitute for human interaction, guidance, and mentorship. The role of educators remains crucial in guiding students, fostering critical thinking, and ensuring the responsible use of AI technologies in education.

The above information obtained from ChatGPT was generated by OpenAI's language model (OpenAI, 2023). And while there was a purpose to using the tool for this section, I personally feel that by using it, I have cheated in some way. How did you feel reading it? Did it sound like me? Or did some part of you recognize the AI imposter in our midst?

In his article in *The New York Times*, "Don't Ban ChatGPT in Schools. Teach With It," technology columnist Kevin Roose comments that he believes "schools should thoughtfully embrace ChatGPT as a teaching aid—one that could unlock student creativity, offer personalized tutoring, and better prepare students to work alongside A. I. systems as adults."

The article addresses how overwhelmed many teachers feel by the idea of monitoring and policing the use of this technology. With so many hours already dedicated to marking student work, the thought of adding even more time to checking whether a student's assignment is the product of their own thoughts and effort, and then calling a meeting with students, parents, and administration to address suspected cheating, is exhausting. Even with technology tools to help teachers identify AI-created work, the time it takes and the emotional effort required to accuse students of misusing tools are so annoying that many may avoid validating student work altogether. This will result in students feeling they have gotten away with it and affirm that it is acceptable to use AI to complete their assignments. Roose asserts that "schools should treat ChatGPT the way they treat calculators—allowing it for some assignments, but not others, and assuming that unless students are being supervised in person with their devices stashed away, they're probably using one."

Love them or hate them, we must acknowledge that ChatGPT and online tech tools are not going away. In fact, as I write this, they are only getting stronger and more abundant. Teachers—*humans*—can not evolve at the rate of technology, but evolve and adapt we must. And yet, even knowing we must change our practices to keep up with our students' needs, our evolution process as an educational community is painfully slow.

I am shocked that more schools and districts have not called for meetings and professional development opportunities to discuss how the educational world is going to adapt to this changing educational landscape. Most of the discussions I have had with colleagues have taken place around the photocopier and have only touched on how shocked we are at AI's capabilities—and how *The Terminator* movie series is starting to feel all too real. As a professional community, educators must work together to understand this technology and help one another become better equipped to teach in a classroom full of tech-savvy students. Although some schools and districts may believe they have addressed the problem by banning the use of AI in school (sound familiar?), that approach is like applying a Band-Aid to a gaping wound. Not only do today's students have access to technology outside the school walls, they will graduate into a world full of generative AI programs. They'll need to know their way around these tools—their strengths and weaknesses, their hallmarks and blind spots—in order to work alongside them. To be good citizens, they'll need hands-on experience to understand how this type of AI works, what types of bias it contains, and how it can be misused and weaponized.

ChatGPT and Me: Chatbots as a Professional Teaching Tool

As I was researching information about ChatGPT, I wanted to challenge the OpenAI model to see if it would help create language around assessment with the proficiency scale and curricular competencies. Many teachers, including myself, have been looking for examples of descriptive language they can use when assessing students that demonstrate proper assessment language in all the areas of the proficiency scale. ChatGPT did not disappoint. The more I used it, the more I began to understand how to better manipulate it and what language prompts I needed to put in to get the results I was looking for . . . and more.

Example Comments for a Student in Spanish at the Developing Level

Communication

- The student is making progress in narrating stories orally, using a wider range of vocabulary and more complex sentence structures.
- The student is starting to respond to questions and instructions with some success, although they still require occasional support.
- The student is becoming more proficient in exchanging ideas and information both orally and in writing, using more varied vocabulary and sentence structures.
- The student is beginning to seek clarification of meaning using common statements and questions but still needs occasional guidance.
- The student is starting to adapt their presentation format to suit their own and others' diverse abilities, although there is room for improvement.

Reading and Comprehension

- The student is making progress in recognizing how the choice of words affects meaning in Spanish, using more varied vocabulary, and showing improved comprehension.
- The student is using language-learning strategies more effectively to increase their understanding and produce oral and written language.
- The student can comprehend key information and supporting details in slow, clear speech and a variety of texts, demonstrating improved reading skills.
- The student is becoming more proficient in comprehending the meaning and viewpoints in stories, although they may still need support with more challenging texts.

Cultural Understanding

- The student is making progress in analyzing regional, cultural, and linguistic practices of various Hispanic communities and their role in shaping cultural identity, showing improved comprehension and insight.
- The student recognizes the importance of story in personal, family, and community identity and can make connections to their own experiences.
- The student is actively engaging in experiences with Hispanic people and communities, broadening their understanding and appreciation of diverse cultures.
- The student is starting to analyze personal, shared, and others' experiences, perspectives, and worldviews through a cultural lens, demonstrating improved critical thinking skills.
- The student is beginning to recognize and appreciate First People's perspectives and knowledge, other ways of knowing, and local cultural knowledge, showing growth in cultural awareness.

The above information obtained from ChatGPT was generated by OpenAI's language model (OpenAI, 2023).

ChatGPT was able to put into words what would have taken me days to write using the exact language that my Ministry of Education has directed me to use. Now, I ask you, am I cheating when I do this? I believe there is very little difference between using these generated prompts for guidance and using others that have been provided for me in an assessment or reporting program. When it comes to using generative AI as a tool, the defining factors for me are how I choose to use these prompts, the time I can save and apply elsewhere, and the ways in which I use the prompts to relay information to students in an individualized manner.

Getting the kinds of prompts I was looking for took some time, tweaking, and manipulation of language. There were moments when I watched the OpenAI blinking and struggling to come up with what I was looking for. Ultimately, we learned to work together, and the results were amazing. I felt like an evil genius! Once I started, I could not be stopped. Together, ChatGPT and I created comment banks that use the language of curricular competencies and proficiency for each of my major projects and assignments in class. All it took was including the parameters that I describe in the instructions of my projects. Below is an example of comments that I could provide as guidance when assessing my students' food and culture projects. I plan to use the below comments as a framework to build individual feedback.

Grade 10 Spanish Food and Culture Project

Emerging Level

Your Spanish food project is at an emerging level. You have made an effort to research a Spanish-speaking country and create a slide show presentation. However, there is room for improvement in organizing your information and effectively presenting it. Keep practicing your research and presentation skills to further develop your project and focus on providing more details and using reliable sources for your research to enhance the overall quality of your project.

Developing Level

You are making steady progress with your Spanish food project. Your research on a Spanish-speaking country is detailed and informative, and your slide show presentation effectively presents the information. Your food truck menu demonstrates an understanding of the country's culinary culture. Continue to strengthen your project by providing clear explanations and incorporating visuals to engage your audience.

Proficient Level

Congratulations on reaching a proficient level with your Spanish food project! Your research on a Spanish-speaking country is comprehensive and well organized, and your slide show presentation effectively communicates the information. Your food truck menu showcases a deep understanding of the country's culinary traditions and culture. Keep up the excellent work, and consider exploring additional elements, such as the incorporation of traditional recipes or the inclusion of interactive elements in your presentation.

Extending Level

Congratulations on your extending level of achievement with your Spanish food project! Your research is meticulous, your presentation captivating. Your food truck menu reflects your creativity and deep understanding of the country's culture and food heritage. You have gone above and beyond in showcasing your knowledge and creativity. Continue to explore additional avenues, such as creating sample dishes or organizing a cultural food fair, to further extend the impact of your project.

> Note that the above descriptions also guide the learners to reach the next level of proficiency and extend their learning journey.

Coming up with creative ways to provide feedback can be a challenge. While I agree that we should be individualizing our assessments, students often have similar things to improve on, and there are only so many ways to say the same thing multiple times. I know I'm not alone. Teachers devote significant time to providing descriptive feedback to our students. Many of us even take the time to write down that feedback, only to notice our work being discarded in the recycling bin on the way out of class.

Using ChatGPT has enabled me to mark and return assignments to students promptly, allowing me more time to speak with my students about their projects on an individual basis. I do not believe that I am cheating. I believe that I am working smarter.

The thing is, I know my students will think the exact same thing when they use this tool to complete an assignment. I also know that if I felt like an evil genius for figuring out how to manipulate ChatGPT to create what I was looking for, my students are inevitably going to succumb to the pull of black hole of OpenAI (if they haven't already) as they try different prompts to see what else the tool is capable of. The difference between me and my students (I like to think) is that I have expertise they do not. Various AI tools can produce content, but it is my expertise that helps me craft prompts and then decide if what ChatGPT generated is appropriate or if I need to work further with it. My skills are still valuable, and so are the skills we need to help our students build.

ADDRESSING TECH WITH YOUR STUDENTS

With your students, take the time at the beginning of the year and times when you assign projects to discuss the technology that exists. Consider dedicating a whole class or lesson series to discussing which tools are available, specifically those that have the potential to impact students' learning. Talk about the advantages and disadvantages of using them, how to navigate them, and what constitutes appropriate and inappropriate use. Yes, I think this is something all teachers should do for any class where technology can affect learning. This is about getting back to the *why* and helping our students to understand how best to navigate and use these tools.

Example Questions for Students to Explore and Discuss

1. What kinds of technology tools exist in the online world?

2. Which tech tools are available to help students specifically with their work in and out of class?
3. In which ways can tech tools help students to learn better?
4. In which ways can tech tools interfere with student learning?
5. When should tech tools be used, and when should they be avoided?
6. When it comes to learning, why should students use tech tools?
7. When it comes to learning, why should students avoid tech tools?
8. Should teachers and schools allow students to use tech tools, and why or why not?
9. Which tech tools can you, as a student, use to help your learning in this specific class or classroom setting?

Approaches to Exploring and Discussing Tech Tools

1. Small-group discussions
2. Full-class debate
3. Inquiry learning project about educational technology

I would include a list of the available tech tools in this book, but by the time this book is published and in your hands, new ones will have surfaced and existing ones may have become outdated. That's why going through the above exercise with your students at the start of each year or semester is a good idea. Students, in most cases, are likely to be more aware of the latest technology out there than we, as teachers, ever will be. If you want to stay current, talk to your students.

Example Questions for Students to Explore and Discuss the Use of OpenAI Technology Generators

1. What are the potential benefits of using AI technology to assist with your work? How can it enhance your learning experience or help you find relevant information?

2. What are the limitations and potential risks of relying heavily on AI technology for your assignments or projects? How might it impact your critical thinking skills or ability to develop your own ideas?
3. How accurate and reliable is the information generated by AI technology? Can you always trust it to provide correct answers, or are there potential biases or errors to consider?
4. How does relying on AI technology for your work affect your personal growth and development? Are you missing out on opportunities to engage with the material, explore different perspectives, or challenge your own thinking?
5. How does using AI technology align with academic integrity? Are there any ethical concerns related to plagiarism, taking credit for work that isn't entirely your own, or presenting information without proper verification?
6. Are there situations where using AI technology may be more appropriate or beneficial than others? How can you strike a balance between utilizing technology and developing your own skills and knowledge?
7. How can you ensure that you're using AI technology as a tool rather than relying on it as a crutch? Which strategies can you implement to maintain your critical thinking abilities and independent thought?
8. Which steps can you take to verify the accuracy of the information that AI technology provides and avoid potential pitfalls?
9. Can you find alternative approaches to using OpenAI that allow you to retain your individuality and personal growth while still benefitting from its capabilities? How can you strike a balance between technology and human engagement in your academic pursuits?

3 WAYS TO HELP STUDENTS NAVIGATE THE ONLINE WORLD

1. Addressing Bias and Misinformation

While we may not be as knowledgeable about the latest and hottest tech that exists in the online world, we are more experienced and knowledgeable when it comes to understanding bias and the world of misinformation. (There is a reason that information, technology, and media literacy courses are being added to the offerings in many educational institutions. I believe they should be a requirement.) Including assignments that have students acknowledge their personal worldview can help them understand how bias is formed. Deliberately examining and contrasting cultural and opposing viewpoints while having open discussions in class will allow students to build their critical thinking skills. Building lessons around misinformation and understanding how to find credible sources will guide students to better identify fake news.

You do not have to do this alone. There are many online resources and pre-built lesson ideas around the topics of misinformation and fake news.

2. Guiding and Providing

There is no way around it. To best help students, we have to become experts ourselves. Set aside some professional development time with your department or teaching buddies to explore and share the online learning tools for your particular subject areas. When you identify great tech tools for students, share them! If you can demonstrate the "best practice" tech tools with your students, they won't go looking for their own in all the wrong places. Spend time showcasing the tools, providing examples, and having students try them out for themselves. In my course syllabus, I often include a link to the online tools that are teacher and district approved for my students to use and tell them that utilizing the right tools in the right ways is not cheating; it is learning smarter. Plus, I always feel pretty smug when I show students tech tools they have never seen before.

3. Going Back to the *Why*

When you and your students understand all the tools that are accessible and how best to utilize them, it is a good idea to discuss the learning advantages and disadvantages of using tech to do the work. Remind students that they are on a learning journey. Have them complete a small exercise to demonstrate the importance and value of doing the work yourself.

Example Exercise

In the boxes below, brainstorm a list of pros and cons about the two ways one can choose to get to the top of the mountain.

Climbing to the Top

PROS	CONS

Getting a Ride to the Top

PROS	CONS

Questions for Thought and Discussion

1. How does the above analogy relate to learning and the use of educational tech tools?
2. How can this analogy be applied to writing an essay?
3. How can this analogy be applied to solving a math problem?
4. Why is the quickest route not always the best route?

PAUSE FOR THOUGHT

1. In which ways have you experienced AI technology like ChatGPT impacting your students and their learning?
2. Do you feel that you understand all the ways in which students can use AI technology to their (dis)advantage in your subject area?
3. In your opinion, does AI technology help or hurt learning?
4. How do you address and navigate the use and misuse of AI technology in your classroom?
5. Have you tried using ChatGPT or a chatbot like it for your own professional purposes? If not, why not? If so, how?

CHAPTER 12

EVALUATING STUDENT WORK
FOCUSING ON PROCESS OVER PRODUCT

Summit (noun): The highest point or peak of a hill or mountain.

Summit (verb): The act of climbing to the top.

When educators assess the full learning journey of their students and include student reflection and response as a part of that process, they value the process over the product. If we think about this as climbing a mountain, with the course end being the top of the mountain, assessing the *product* would look like assessing how quickly, efficiently, and effectively each student got to the top. Assessing the *process* would take into account everything that happened along the way. What skill development occurred, and what was learned? Which obstacles were overcome, and how? Which routes were taken to reach the end?

I believe the product is important and absolutely has a place in assessment, as it drives the process. In a world of OpenAI technologies and increasing availability and capability of tech tools that can produce the final product, however, we must consider where the main weight of our assessment lies (possible pun intended). If a final essay is worth 10, 20, or 30 percent of a grade, should 100 percent of that be dedicated to the final product, which could have been generated with the help of OpenAI? Or would breaking down the process and evaluating the gains at each stage—development, research, writing, and editing—provide a more inclusive view of the student's achievement? In keeping with the mountain analogy, wherein our course end is the summit, we might consider that valuing the process over the product (emphasizing the verb use of *summit* rather than the noun) provides a more holistic view of summative assessment.

TIERED-ASSESSMENT STRATEGIES IN A WORLD OF AI

Receiving an AI-generated piece of writing or work from a student is frustrating. It can even feel like an insult given the work you've put into teaching. It's as if the student is saying, "I don't like what you have asked me to do," or "I don't think what we are doing is important enough." When we face these moments, we may wonder if what we are doing is a waste of time.

Diversifying assessment allows for differentiated instruction and can provide students with choice and flexibility. It may also be a way for teachers and students to work with and accept AI in a manner that can still promote student growth and learning, leading to less frustration on both sides. Let's go back to the mountain!

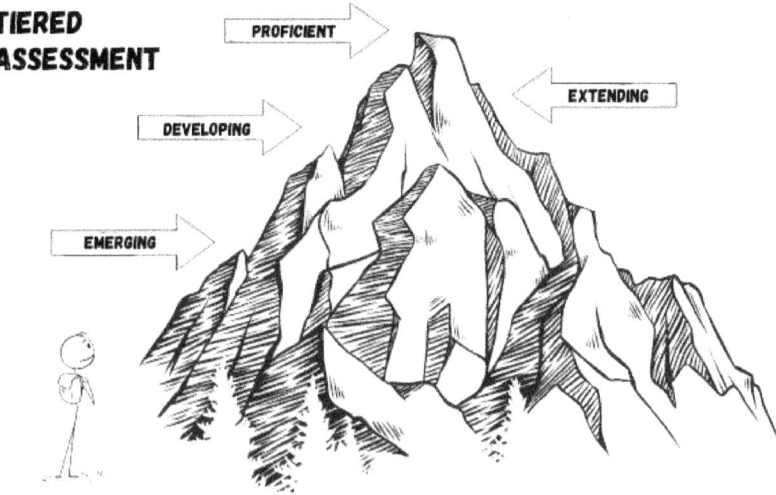

Breaking down assignments into tiers defined by student proficiency allows us to offer differentiation and better accessibility to learning for all. Completion of the assignment at the proficient level may be the goal of many students, but the idea of completing the assignment to achieve this can feel so overwhelming that they choose to use AI to help them get there.

If I were asked to run a marathon or climb Mt. Everest this week, I couldn't do it. I wouldn't even want to try. This may seem like a weird analogy, but for some of our students, writing a full essay feels just as harrowing. They see the task as something so insurmountable, they don't even want to attempt it.

I may not be able to complete a marathon right now, but I could run 10K, and shouldn't that be worth something? Could I eventually run a full marathon if I put in the time and work? Could I do it if I had a training program that broke it down into smaller steps to reach the bigger goal? I would like to think I could. At the very least, I would be willing to try.

Breaking down assignments into smaller proficiency levels allows for the necessary skills to be developed, one small assignment step at a time. It also allows students the opportunity to reach new levels, knowing that along the way, they are building the skills to reach whatever goals they set for themselves next, be it meeting the emerging, developing, proficient, or extending level. When teachers and students are clear on the skills needed to acquire the various levels of proficiency for a specific assignment, students are better able to see a defined path between the proficiency levels and can proceed towards their personalized goals with confidence.

This tier-assessment approach can acknowledge the existence of AI and allow students to use it in a responsible and targeted manner that still encourages skill building. Furthermore, by acknowledging the existence of AI, teachers are working with students to help them understand both the potential advantages and disadvantages of its use, ideally guiding them to make responsible decisions for themselves.

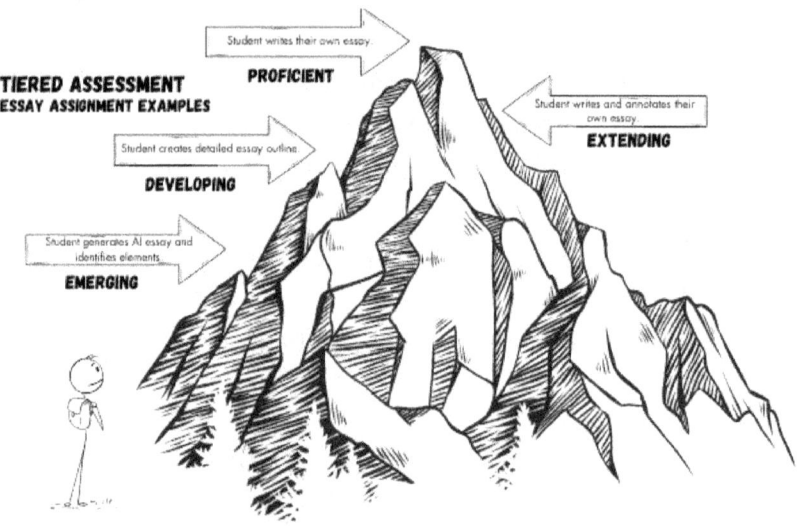

Essay Writing Example—Tiered Assessment

Emerging Level—The student works with AI to generate an essay that they then use to identify elements of essay structure. They could also point out the essay's strengths/weaknesses and the various ways in which the essay connects to the overall goals of the assignment.

Developing Level—The student creates a detailed essay outline that includes elements defined by the teacher, such as thesis statement, paragraph structure, etc.

Proficient Level—The student writes the essay, connecting to the goals of the assignment.

Extending Level—The student writes and annotates their essay. The student writes an essay using a higher level of descriptive language. The student exceeds the goals of the assignment in a definable way.

With the tiered-proficiency levels provided, if a student still feels the need to hand in an AI-generated essay in hopes of reaching the proficient level, then a longer conversation is needed to find out why these choices were made.

PAUSE FOR THOUGHT

1. What does the mountain summit look like in your own courses?
2. Which "products" represent the successful completion of your course?
3. How can the products of your course be broken down to place a higher value on the process?
4. Which skills are students developing in their process work?
5. In which ways do you (or can you) accurately assess the skills students are developing during their process work?
6. Are your current rubrics or assessment tools placing more emphasis on rewarding the product or the process?
7. In what ways can students work with AI while still reaching a level on the proficiency scale?

A CHATGPT PROMPTED ANECDOTE ABOUT THE MISUSE OF TECHNOLOGY

ICARUS AND ALEX

Once upon a time, in a world where technology and mythology intertwined, there was a young student named Alex. Alex was known for an insatiable curiosity and love for exploration. One day, they stumbled upon an ancient Greek myth about a boy named Icarus and his wings made of feathers and wax.

Intrigued by the story, Alex's imagination ignited. They couldn't help but wonder if there were any parallels between Icarus's tale and the modern technology they used every day. Soon, their attention turned to ChatGPT, an advanced large language model (LLM) capable of answering questions and engaging in conversations.

Driven by curiosity, Alex decided to have a conversation with ChatGPT. They started asking various questions, seeking knowledge and guidance. The model responded with astonishing accuracy, captivating Alex's attention. It became a habit for Alex to turn to ChatGPT for answers to every question they encountered.

Over time, Alex's reliance on ChatGPT grew stronger. They no longer bothered to think critically or seek alternative sources of information. The more Alex depended on the technology, the more they detached themselves from the world around them.

As days turned into weeks, Alex's relationships began to suffer. Friends and family felt ignored as Alex prioritized conversations with ChatGPT over human interaction. Their once inquisitive and independent mind became enslaved by the convenience of instant information.

Caught in this vicious cycle, Alex experienced plummeting grades, and Alex's passion for learning faded away. They had become a mere vessel for the technology, their own thoughts and creativity stifled by the constant reliance on ChatGPT.

One day, Alex's closest friend, Sarah, noticed the drastic change in behaviour. Concerned, Sarah confronted Alex about their excessive reliance on technology. She reminded Alex of the myth of Icarus, recounting how he flew too close to the sun and met his tragic end. Sarah drew parallels between Icarus' downfall and Alex's own surrender to the technology's control.

Touched by Sarah's words, Alex realised the truth in her analogy. They had indeed become like Icarus, carried away by an infatuation with ChatGPT. Overwhelmed with regret, Alex acknowledged the damage caused by excessive reliance on the technology and the toll it had taken on their life.

With newfound determination, Alex vowed to break free from the clutches of ChatGPT. They sought guidance from their teachers and mentors, rediscovering the joy of learning through human connections and critical thinking. Day by day, Alex slowly regained control of their life, reclaiming their independence and creativity.

In this tale, the story of Icarus and the overpowering influence of technology served as a cautionary reminder for Alex. They learned that while technology can offer incredible benefits, surrendering oneself entirely to its control can have dire consequences. With newfound wisdom, Alex embarked on a journey of self-discovery, embracing a balanced approach to technology and rediscovering the beauty of human connections in the process.

The End

Written by OpenAI (with prompts from me), 2023.

FULLY ADAPTING TO THE ADVANCING TECH

While some educational facilities are choosing to ban the use of ChatGPT and other OpenAI technologies or think that they are banning it when their students can access it in other ways, I am asserting that educators should embrace and teach the skills that are necessary for proper and effective use—skills that are and will continue to be highly beneficial and sought after in the workplace.

I know not everyone holds the same opinion. This is a controversial topic. If you are staunchly against having your students use chatbots, I completely understand where you are coming from. I welcome you to stick to your convictions and skip this section.

I asked ChatGPT what skills are needed for the proper and effective use of its platform, and here is what it shared:

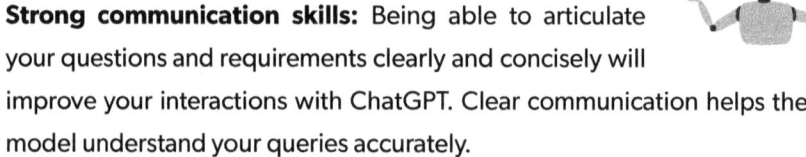

Strong communication skills: Being able to articulate your questions and requirements clearly and concisely will improve your interactions with ChatGPT. Clear communication helps the model understand your queries accurately.

Critical thinking: ChatGPT is an AI model, and it's important to critically evaluate the responses it generates. Consider the context, relevance, and accuracy of the information provided. Critical thinking allows you to make informed judgments about the responses and use them appropriately.

Domain knowledge: Having a solid understanding of the subject matter or domain you're discussing can greatly enhance your interactions with ChatGPT. Providing specific and relevant information will help the model generate more accurate and meaningful responses.

Experimentation and exploration: ChatGPT is a tool that can assist with a wide range of tasks. Experimenting with different approaches and exploring the model's capabilities can help you understand its strengths and limitations. This can involve trying different prompts, phrasing questions differently, or even asking the model to generate creative content.

Patience and adaptability: While ChatGPT is a powerful large language model, it may occasionally provide inaccurate or irrelevant responses. Having patience and adapting your questions or prompts can help you get better results. Iterating and refining your queries based on the model's feedback will improve the quality of the responses.

Ethical considerations: Large language models like ChatGPT should be used responsibly and ethically. Understand the potential biases and limitations of AI tools, and be cautious about relying solely on their responses. Consider the source and verify information whenever necessary.

Familiarity with the model's strengths and limitations: Being aware of the capabilities and limitations of ChatGPT will help you set realistic expectations. GPT-3.5, for example, has been trained on a wide range of internet text, but it may not have knowledge of recent events or specific details beyond its training cutoff date.

Remember, ChatGPT is a tool to assist you, and combining its outputs with your own knowledge and expertise can lead to the best results (OpenAI, 2023).

Example Skill-Building Activities Using Chatbots

(Best used in a humanities class)

1. **Analyze:** Have a chatbot create an essay on a chosen topic and have students analyze, critique, and mark the essay as if they were a teacher.

2. **Outline or Rough Draft:** Have students use a chatbot to create an initial introduction, outline, or full rough draft of their essay. Then have students use the creation as a jumping-off point to flesh out their actual essay. I have yet to see a chatbot properly cite quotations, so this can be a good activity to have students insert supporting quotations to bolster a weak argument.
3. **Compare and Contrast:** Have students read a chatbot-created essay and a real well-sourced essay on the same topic. Students can brainstorm and discuss the merits of a soundly constructed and cited essay written by a proper creator.
4. **Manipulate it:** Give students an essay topic Have them use a chatbot to write it. Have them guide and manipulate the chatbot to write a unique essay, unlike any other that another student will hand in. Then have students compare their essays to view the similarities and differences in the chatbot's final work.

I understand that having students learn how to manipulate chatbots to write essays feels like playing with fire. We fear we may burn down the whole building. The reality is that our students already have access to the matches and fuel; what they need is supervision. They will use AI—with or without educational guidance. News outlets, companies, and professionals around the world are already using chatbots in various ways. We very well could soon see "experience with chatbots" or "proficient in chatbot language" as a qualification in job descriptions. We cannot know the future, but where and when we can, we should be teaching our students to function in the world they are going to be living in, not just the world they live in now . . . or worse, the one we grew up in.

CHAPTER 13

PUT IT INTO PRACTICE

APPLICATIONS FOR SCHOOLS, TEACHERS, PARENTS, AND SOCIETY

Creating this book has led me down a path I wasn't expecting and never intended in my teaching career. Like the main character in *Alice in Wonderland*, I feel as if I have gone through the looking glass, and I am navigating a new reality with corporate companies like Meta playing the role of the Queen of Hearts. Books with topics about advancing technology, lost focus, rising rates of anxiety, and living in a digital world now line my shelves and curate my online search engines. Experts all seem to have research data and opinions that warn of the dangers of this new digital era, and yet so very few offer any real applications for how to teach and prepare the youth growing up with it.

Many are shouting for outright smartphone or technology bans in schools, which parts of me can align with. We will never ban this technology from the world, though, and therefore, a better approach is to educate and regulate (which I like, perhaps because it rhymes). When we have information and we know more, we tend to make better decisions.

While I have included many techniques, tips, and ideas for helping students learn in this new era of technology, I feel as if an important step is to implement a whole new course in schools. Teachers (and parents) must educate students and children about how to navigate and understand the world they are growing up in.

In this bonus section, written in the final editing phase of this book, I am including ideas for courses and lessons that can be implemented or woven into existing courses at the junior and senior levels of school. While some of these suggestions may seem obvious, according to discussions with my students, many of these concepts have never been covered or discussed in school or with parents. My hope is that by implementing these ideas, some of the negative impacts—such as increased difficulties with focus, anxiety, feelings of depression and loneliness, and a lack of empathy—that teachers are witnessing in the classroom will be mitigated.

COURSE AND LESSON IDEAS FOR GRADES 7, 8, AND 9

With grades 7, 8, and 9 being the years in which many youths are begging their parents (and which many parents are giving in) for a smartphone, these preteens must understand the power of the technology they are about to have in their hands. Before people are allowed to drive, they must study and complete a test to obtain a licence. I am not advocating a written exam before they get a smartphone; however, I do think some mandatory education is imperative. You may think that some of these concepts seem too advanced for preteens to understand. My rebuttal to that is to ask you to think about the ramifications of putting a device into their young hands that they cannot fully understand.

The following concepts could be taught as a separate exploratory/elective course or in a larger assembly, although a smaller setting is preferable.

The Basics

Introduction to Technology—Cover basic concepts like what technology is, different types of technology students will encounter in daily life, and its impact on society.

Digital Citizenship—Demonstrate the responsible use of technology, including online safety, etiquette, and respecting others' digital privacy.

Internet Safety—Focus on teaching students about safe internet browsing habits, avoiding online predators, and recognizing and reporting inappropriate content. Understand how to set privacy settings on social media accounts.

Socializing in an Online World

Digital Communication Etiquette—Explore positive digital communication etiquette when interacting with others online, including using respectful language, tone, and behaviour. The potential consequences of inappropriate or hurtful online communication, such as cyberbullying, misunderstandings, and damage to relationships. Emphasize the value of building positive and meaningful relationships online by connecting with friends, family, and peers in supportive and respectful ways.

Balancing Life in the Online and In-person World—Encourage students to strike a healthy balance between their online and offline social interactions, recognizing the importance of face-to-face communication and real-life relationships.

Responsible Social Media Use—Teach students about responsible social media use, including the impact of their online posts and contributions on themselves and others. Discuss the importance of thinking before posting and considering the potential consequences and implications of sharing content online.

Managing Online Conflict and Disagreements—Help students understand how online conflicts can arise. Provide strategies for students to navigate online conflicts and disagreements constructively, and how to seek compromise or resolution instead of avoiding the situation. Teach students how to recognize and respond to cyberbullying behaviour, including when to seek help from a trusted adult.

Managing Screentime

The Impacts of Screen Time—Show students how to monitor and check their screen time. Discuss the potential risks of excessive screen time and social media use, such as decreased physical activity, sleep disturbances, and feelings of loneliness or isolation. Guide students to brainstorm to recognize the negative impacts of too much screen time and healthier alternatives for social interactions.

Better Understand the Technology—Teach students about the addictive nature of technology and how it affects the brain's reward system, similar to substances like drugs and alcohol. Teach how the infinite scroll, "likes," and app streaks contribute to screen time. Help students understand the negative impacts of excessive technology use on their physical health, mental health, relationships, and academic performance.

The Emotional Impacts of Social Networking Apps—To better understand themselves and their emotions, help students understand how social networking sites can make them feel. Discuss how getting "likes" or followers makes them feel and how it influences their use of the app.

Strategies for Self-Regulation—Teach students to monitor their technology use by keeping track of their screen time, identifying patterns and triggers for excessive use, and reflecting on the impact of technology on their well-being. Help students develop coping strategies for managing stress and negative emotions without turning to technology, such as deep breathing, mindfulness meditation, journaling, or engaging in creative activities.

Building Better Habits

Creating Tech-Free Zones—Encourage students to designate certain areas in their homes (e.g., bedrooms) and times of the day (e.g., mealtimes, before bedtime) as tech-free zones to promote face-to-face interaction and instill positive patterns.

Mindful Technology Use—Promote mindfulness practices such as taking regular breaks from screens, being present and attentive during in-person interactions, and paying attention to how technology use makes them feel emotionally and physically.

Approaches to Learning and Study—Discuss how smartphones can impact attentiveness, focus, and the ability to take in information. Highlight the benefits of being present. Guide students to put their phones on silent and out of sight when learning or studying.

Promote Hobbies and Physical Activity—Emphasize the importance of having hobbies and engaging in regular physical activity and outdoor play as alternatives to sedentary screen time. Encourage students to explore offline activities and interests that they enjoy and that provide a sense of fulfillment and accomplishment.

COURSE IDEAS FOR GRADES 10, 11, AND 12

By their senior years, students have had their phones and have been growing more accustomed to navigating a world of rapidly advancing technology, social networks, and generative AI tools. They are able to comprehend and understand advanced concepts and have a growing need to understand themselves. For them, these years are crucial for learning about the complexities of a tech-driven world and its impacts on society. Among other things, how we work, learn, socialize, and navigate relationships have all been impacted by technology.

Young adults will one day be making decisions and voting for policies and politicians that can have tremendous impacts on the world. Social networking and app algorithms can influence how, what, and why we think certain things. To be an informed citizen of the world, teens should be better taught to understand how both they and the world are shaped through a technological lens.

First, I will introduce a possible course that can implemented at the high school level, something I think all districts should be providing or using to update older courses such as Media Literacy or New Media. Then, I will suggest lessons and activities that can be woven into core subject areas. The more schools educate about these topics, the more positive impacts they can have on our teens.

Disclaimer: I do not consider myself to be the guru of all things tech and media, but I am a trained high school teacher with a Master's degree in Work, Organization, and Leadership with a keen interest in helping teachers. I feel the frustration of my colleagues, and I see the struggles of my students as the world has rapidly changed with smartphones and technology. What I do not yet see are the adaptations and implementations that should be made at the educational level. Perhaps these are all coming, or perhaps, like most, we are waiting for someone else to come up with an idea or tell us what to do. Please, take what you think is useful or use what you can as building blocks for something greater, and pass it on.

Possible Course Names

- Digital Connections: Exploring Tech, Society, and Self
- Navigating the Technological World
- Digital Studies
- Tech and Humanity

Course Overview

The course will help students to better understand the digital world by examining the sociological and psychological impacts of technology, offering students a deeper understanding of how it shapes human behaviour and social interactions. The course will also provide a practical introduction to understanding app development and the Attention Economy, inspiring students to think creatively and critically about the digital tools they use every day. By examining the effects of technology on brain development and mastering self-regulation strategies, students will have an understanding of themselves and be better equipped to maintain their digital well-being.

Unit Overview

Unit 1—Introduction to Navigating a Technological World

Introduce students to the foundational concepts and trends shaping the modern technological landscape, fostering a broad understanding of technology's role in society. Educate students about potential online risks and threats, empowering them with strategies to stay safe, secure, and responsible in their online activities.

Unit 2—Social Media and Online Communication

Explore the impact of social media on communication, relationships, and society, while fostering critical thinking and digital citizenship skills in online interactions.

Unit 3—Digital Citizenship and Ethics

Foster an understanding of ethical and responsible behaviour in the digital world, emphasizing the importance of digital citizenship and contributing positively to online communities. Explore how corporations approach these topics.

Unit 4—Media Literacy and Fake News

Develop students' critical thinking and media literacy skills to discern credible sources from misinformation, equipping them to navigate the complex media landscape with discernment and skepticism.

Unit 5: Generative Artificial Intelligence

Introduce students to the concepts and applications of generative AI tools like ChatGPT, sparking curiosity and understanding of these transformative technologies. Discuss themes related to responsible uses of the technologies and their impacts on personal development and learning. Explore the creative potential of generative AI technologies through inquiry, inspiring students to harness AI tools for artistic and individual expression.

Unit 6—Sociology of Technology and Social Networks

Examine the social and cultural implications of technological advancements, fostering critical reflection on technology's impact—particularly social networking sites like Instagram and Snapchat—on society and human behaviour. How do algorithms work? Why are algorithms used?

Unit 7—Psychology of Technology and Self-Understanding

Deepen students' self-awareness and understanding of the psychological effects of technology and social media use on themselves and others.

Unit 8—The Developing Brain and Impacts of Technology

Investigate the intersection of neuroscience and technology, exploring how technology and social networking sites influence brain development and cognition in adolescents.

Unit 9—Digital Well-Being and Self-Regulation

Promote strategies for maintaining balance and well-being in a digital world, empowering students to develop self-regulation skills and cultivate healthy relationships with and through technology.

Unit 10—App Development and the Attention Economy

Inspire students to explore the world of app development and understand the Attention Economy, fostering creativity, critical thinking, and ethical considerations in designing digital experiences.

Unit 11—Advancing Technology and the Future

Explore emerging technologies such as virtual reality (VR), augmented reality (AR), and other cutting-edge innovations, examining their potential to transform various industries and everyday life. Students will examine future possibilities of advancing tech and the societal, ethical, and practical implications of their widespread adoption.

Curricular Outcomes

Understanding Technology and Society—Demonstrate an understanding of the historical and current impacts of technology on society. Explore the relationship between technology and socioeconomic factors.

Digital Literacy—Develop skills to critically evaluate digital content for accuracy, credibility, and bias. Apply effective strategies for managing and organizing digital information.

Technology and Personal Well-being—Identify the psychological effects of technology on personal well-being. Implement strategies for maintaining a healthy balance between technology use and personal life.

Ethical Use of Technology—Recognize ethical considerations related to technology use, including privacy, security, and digital citizenship. Evaluate the implications of technology on individual rights and freedoms.

Emerging Technologies—Explore emerging technologies such as virtual reality, augmented reality, and artificial intelligence. Assess the potential impacts of emerging technologies on society and individual lives.

> For a free full course package with more lessons and ideas, please visit my website: heretolearn.ca

INTEGRATING TECHNOLOGY-FOCUSED LESSONS INTO CORE COURSES

English

Analyzing Online Texts—Have students analyze articles, blogs, and social media posts for credibility, bias, and persuasive techniques.

Nonfiction Analysis—Choose texts that focus on understanding how technology and social networking can impact brain development or social-emotional well-being.

Character Analysis and Social Media—Create fake social media profiles for literary characters, exploring how they might present themselves online and how this may be different from how they present themselves in real life.

Comparative Essays—Have students write essays comparing their own experiences on social media with those of characters in novels or stories.

Writing Activities—Encourage students to write personal essays reflecting on their own experiences with technology, social media, and their psychological impact. Use journaling prompts related to themes of self-identity, stress, and resilience as explored through literature.

Technology in Dystopian Literature—Discuss the role of technology in societies depicted in dystopian novels. Draw parallels to real-world technological issues.

Ethics of Technology—Hold debates on topics such as privacy, digital surveillance, or the psychological impact of social media, encouraging critical thinking and persuasive speaking skills.

Inquiry-Based Projects—Have students create inquiry projects that explore themes within technology and society. Themes could include the developing brain and technology, generative AI, advancing technology with virtual reality, sociology, and social networking, etc.

Movie Units—Example: *The Matrix* examines the control exerted by technology over human lives and the ideas that perception can be manipulated and reality may be a construct. Students could further explore the sociological implications of control in the world of *The Matrix*. Provide questions for students to consider around themes of identity formation and transformation.

Sciences

Digital Tools in Science—Use digital tools and software for collecting and analyzing data in experiments (e.g., spreadsheets, graphing tools, sensors, and data loggers). Incorporate virtual labs and simulations to demonstrate scientific concepts and experiments that may be difficult to perform in a traditional lab setting.

Emerging Technologies—Discuss emerging technologies such as AI, CRISPR, and nanotechnology. Have students research and present on the potential impacts of these technologies. Study how advancements in technology, such as telemedicine and wearable health monitors, are transforming healthcare and the possible impacts.

Societal Impact of Science—Explore the ethical implications of scientific advancements, such as genetic engineering, cloning, and climate engineering. Discuss how scientific discoveries and technological advancements have historically impacted society and culture.

Cognitive Science and Learning—Teach students about the biology of the brain and how it relates to behaviour, learning, and memory. Further, explore these themes in relation to social media and influencing techniques used by app designers.

Health and Well-Being—Discuss the psychological effects of stress, sleep, and exercise on overall health. Include the impact of technology on mental health, such as screen time, social media usage, and the psychological implications of living in a tech-driven world.

Behavioural Experiments—Conduct simple experiments to study human behaviour and cognition, such as memory tests, reaction-time experiments, or surveys on technology use.

Scientific Literature—Read and analyze peer-reviewed papers that explore themes surrounding science, technology, psychology, brain development, etc. Or have students lead their own experiment or inquiry project and write a paper on their own findings.

Maths

Social Networks and Graph Theory—Introduce students to graph theory through the study of social networks, examining how people are connected and how information spreads.

Cognitive and Behavioural Statistics—Study how mathematical models explain human decision-making processes and economic behaviours.

Probability and Decision Making—Introduce basic concepts of game theory to understand strategic interactions in competitive situations and have students explore how this is used in app development.

Research Projects—Have students undertake research projects that combine mathematical analysis with sociological or psychological data. For example, analyzing the correlation between studying and sleep patterns in relation to social media usage. Students can explore mathematical concepts and their applications in technology, sociology, or psychology.

PROFESSIONAL DEVELOPMENT FOR EDUCATORS

While this book is a good place to start, I encourage professional development around these themes for educators at all levels. As technology advances, so must we. Here are some ideas to implement with educators in your school. This could be full-staff professional development, department-focused, or simply a group of teachers who want to have a book club and bounce ideas off one another.

Understanding Today's Student—Engage in learning sessions that explore understanding how technology, social media, and other factors have shaped cognitive development, attention spans, and learning behaviours.

The Brain of Today's Student—Examine insights into the neuroscience behind Generation Z's brain development, focusing on topics such as neuroplasticity, attentional processes, and the impact of digital media on brain functioning.

Attention Management Strategies—Educators could explore strategies for managing and enhancing Generation Z's attention in the classroom, including techniques for minimizing distractions, promoting sustained focus, and integrating engaging and interactive activities into lessons. This might involve exploring mindfulness practices, brain breaks, and technology integration strategies that optimize learning and attention. It could also include techniques such as setting clear expectations, minimizing distractions, chunking information, and providing frequent feedback.

Habit Formation Techniques—Educators could learn about the science of habit formation and how to apply it to classroom routines and student behaviours. They could further explore ways to help students develop positive habits related to organization, time management, study skills, and digital device use.

Optimizing the Learning Environment—Educators could explore "habit cueing" and how to create a physical and psychological learning environment that supports Generation Z students' focus, well-being, and academic success.

Technology Management Strategies—This is important for both the educators and the students. Explore techniques for setting boundaries around technology use in the classroom, implementing digital detox periods, and teaching students self-regulation strategies for managing screen time and device use.

School Practices and Strategies—Educators could work together to brainstorm and implement strategies for digital wellness programs, tech-free zones and times, personal health and wellness in relation to tech use, parent involvement and education, and intervention strategies for students who display behavioural addictive tendencies.

Working in a Tech-Driven World—Educators could discuss the implications, both positive and negative, of working in a technology-heavy environment. Strategies could be cultivated to help teachers manage their workload and digital practices in relation to their mental health and well-being.

Most importantly, educators must feel supported by parents, administrators, and society. They should be given time for professional development in these areas in order to catch up with recent technological developments that directly impact their own practice and the students they teach.

CHAPTER 14

MY FINAL THOUGHTS ON OPEN AI AND TECHNOLOGY

When I first had the idea to work on an educational methods book that addresses smartphones and technology, ChatGPT had not hit the internet. By the time this book is in your hands, I have no idea what else will be out or what the technology will be capable of. As a teacher in this technological world, it's hard not to feel like I'm behind the times no matter how many articles I read, interviews I watch, or podcasts I listen to. I'm not alone in my concerns about where and how fast we are travelling down this road. Even the inventors of this technology are sounding the alarm about its potential capabilities and warning governments to apply regulations or halt AI development altogether.

The students we teach today were born into a world of smartphones. Their adeptness with technology makes AI seem like the next logical step to them, not the giant leap it feels like for some of us in older generations. Even if we may think we know better than our students, we cannot blame them for feeling so comfortable with the high-tech world that is completely normal for them. Beyond that, we can't deny that technology offers us some great benefits. If someone gave me the option of contacting a friend in another country via a "snail mail" letter, an email, or a text message, I would likely choose the most efficient way and send a text. Knowing my options and the delight of receiving a physical card in the mail, however, might make snail mail a valid or even better choice on occasion.

Every generation advances, and every earlier generation must adapt from the world they knew to the world they know while still teaching the younger generations important lessons from the past. In researching and using ChatGPT to better understand it, I fell under its spell as I watched it magically create the words that I and others in my profession have been lacking when it comes to assessing with the proficiency scale. At first, I opposed the idea of using it to create any content for this book. I later decided to use it to create parts of the section about it, specifically to help those who have not yet seen its capabilities better understand how it can be used in a professional capacity. I also wanted to demonstrate what we as teachers need to be doing to help our students navigate its platform.

It's time, perhaps past time, to reinvent a curriculum that helps students build and harness durable skills that transcend technology. Durable skills, often known as soft skills, are things like critical thinking, problem-solving, communication, collaboration, creativity, adaptability, leadership, and teamwork—to name a few. These are the skills that may be most in jeopardy when students defer to using AI tools to do their work. We must find ways to teach these skills and convince our students that honing these abilities is worth the time and effort. Generative AI is a seismic shift that has completely changed the landscape of education and the working world. Teachers must adapt, and we require time and training to do it.

I never thought I would be using *The Terminator* franchise or the allusion to Skynet to help my students understand the potential pitfalls of this technological advancement. Neither would I have ever imagined that those fictional examples would become common analogies used by news media programs. Yet here we are. While technology may be making work easier, it emphasizes the importance of education for all of society. Students today need to understand the potential risks of having unlimited access to misinformation and disinformation as well as the significant role that algorithms play in determining what content we see and how those algorithms can impact the greater society. In my opinion, all youth should take a required course called Social Media and Me, which covers the psychology of social media and how it can be used to curate addictive tendencies, manipulate emotions, create a false sense of reality, and influence the formation of an individual's identity.

Finally, and probably the most important thing parents and teachers can do to help our children and teens manage the technology in their hands, is to educate and guide them away from abusing it. We need to show this iGen the mental and emotional benefits of putting the phone away and actively engaging with the world and the people around them.

REWILDING AND GETTING OUTSIDE

While much of this book has discussed the ways in which educators can better navigate the technologically inundated classroom space, where smartphones are seemingly melded into student's hands, I would like to finish with what I think is the most important thing we could be guiding our students to do: turn it off, put it down, and get outside. Obviously, if it were as simple as that, there would be no point in writing this book.

According to a recent article about "Why Kids Need to Spend Time in Nature," published by the Child Mind Institute, "the average American child spends [less than 7 minutes a day] playing outside and over 7 hours a day in front of a screen." No matter where you look for the information, all statistics point to the fact that kids are spending more time staring at a screen and less time outside and physically interacting with others. This shift has come at a pace that our biological evolution can not keep up with. Quite simply, we are not built for the world we are currently living in, nor will we ever be, and recognizing this has led to a societal panic about kids spending too much time indoors and a crisis that has been coined a *nature deficit disorder*. Traditional Western systems of schooling deemphasize the importance of getting outside as students get older, which has largely contributed to the situation we are currently in.

I like to think of myself as an innovative and creative teacher who provides interesting activities to engage my students with their learning. Today, being *innovative* and *current* usually means going paperless, which can equal the use of online tools, which means I, too, am guilty of putting more screens in front of my students. The global pandemic added to the problem by catapulting our lives online (in some cases necessarily). Despite being aware of the dangers, I do not see myself or anyone else going back to prescriptive textbooks and workbooks or lessening the use of technology. But I refuse to be apathetic about the risky realities of the world we live and teach in.

Today's generation does not know a world where smartphones are not intrinsically attached to almost every activity. We cannot expect students to understand what they are missing out on unless we give them the opportunity to experience it, which may not be easy. The classroom is a comfortable, warm, and safe environment that provides an enclosed space to easily keep an eye on our students. Going outside can present challenges, requires guardian or administrative approval, and depending on where you live, be infeasible, unsafe, or uncomfortable. However, it would be irresponsible of educators to not provide students with as many opportunities as possible to interact with one another and their environment.

Today, multiple movements seek to inspire people to get outside, including forest bathing and *rewilding*. The intentions of these experiences are to, among other things, get people closer to nature and to the brain by temporarily eliminating the stimulus of modern society. In an ideal world, outdoor education classes would be a mandatory part of the curriculum and a required course for graduation. I do not believe this is an extreme suggestion. I believe it is critical. With kids spending less time outdoors, they are becoming more disconnected from their natural environment, which, when considering the current climate crisis, could not come at a worse time.

So, what can we as educators do? Whatever we can. Here are a few ideas:

- **Educate students** about the psychological, physical, and mental health benefits of being outside and connecting with the environment.
- **Implement Walk and Talks** that pair students together to discuss guided questions. The only rule is that they are not allowed to go on their phones.
- **Explore Place-Based Education Practices** with your colleagues and departments.
- **Encourage environmental stewardship** by participating in activities that promote conservation and ecosystem revitalization.
- **Lead by example** by dedicating professional development days to being outside. Organize staff walks, hikes, kayaking experiences, game days, etc.

PAUSE FOR THOUGHT

1. Which outdoor areas of your school or neighbourhood could function well as alternative learning spaces?
2. How can some of your lessons or activities be adapted to get students outside?

3. How can you and your students become better stewards of the environment that surrounds your school? *Bonus points for connecting this to curricular outcomes.

I can't think of a better way to end this book than by encouraging you and your students and children to get outside. Which is what you should do. Please put this down and go enjoy the outside world. Leave your phone behind.

GLOSSARY OF TECHNOLOGY

TERMS ALL TEACHERS AND PARENTS OF TEENS SHOULD KNOW

App (Application)—A software program designed to perform specific tasks or functions on a computer or mobile device

Artificial Intelligence (AI)—The simulation of human intelligence by computer systems, including learning, reasoning, and problem-solving capabilities

Bias—Prejudice or favouritism towards a particular group, individual, or point of view, often influencing the presentation or interpretation of information

Confirmation Bias—The tendency to seek out, interpret, and remember information that confirms one's pre-existing beliefs or biases, while ignoring or discounting contradictory evidence

Cyberbullying—Bullying or harassment that takes place over digital devices or online platforms, including social media, email, or text messages

Cybersecurity—Measures taken to protect computer systems and networks from unauthorized access, data breaches, and cyber attacks

Data Privacy—The protection of personal information and the right of individuals to control the collection and use of their data

Digital Citizenship—The responsible and ethical use of technology, including respecting others' privacy, practicing online safety, and contributing positively to online communities

Digital Detox—A period of time during which a person refrains from using digital devices or engaging in online activities

Digital Divide—The gap between individuals or communities that have access to digital technologies and those that do not, often due to socioeconomic factors

Digital Footprint—The trail of data left behind by a person's online activity, including social media posts, website visits, and online purchases

Digital Literacy—The ability to access, understand, evaluate, and create digital content using various digital technologies and tools

Digital Native—A person who has grown up using digital technology from a young age, often more comfortable and adept at using technology compared to digital immigrants

Digital Well-Being—Maintaining a healthy balance and mindful use of technology to promote physical, mental, and emotional well-being

Echo Chamber—A situation in which individuals are exposed only to information and opinions that reinforce their existing beliefs, leading to polarization and the amplification of extreme viewpoints

Endless Scroll—A design feature used in websites and apps where content continuously loads as the user scrolls down the page, making it difficult to find a natural stopping point and often leading to prolonged usage

Ethical Use of Technology—Using technology in a morally responsible manner, considering the impact on others and society as a whole

Fake News—False or misleading information presented as news, often spread through social media or other online platforms

Filter Bubble—The personalized online environment created by algorithms that selectively present information based on a user's past behaviour and preferences, potentially limiting exposure to diverse perspectives

Generative AI—AI technology capable of generating new content, such as text, images, or music, based on input data or patterns

Internet—A global network of interconnected computers and other devices that communicate using standardized protocols

Media Convergence—The merging of traditional media (e.g., print, television) with digital technologies (e.g., internet, social media) to create new forms of media content and communication

Media Literacy—The ability to access, analyze, evaluate, and create media in various forms, including print, digital, and social media

Online Communication—Communication conducted over the internet, including email, instant messaging, and video conferencing

Operating System (OS)—Software that manages computer hardware and provides common services for computer programs

Privacy Settings—Controls and options provided by websites, apps, and devices to manage the privacy of personal information and online activities

Search Engine—A web-based tool that allows users to search for information on the internet by entering keywords or phrases in a web browser

Self-Regulation—The ability to control one's thoughts, emotions, and behaviours in order to achieve goals and maintain well-being, including regulating technology use

Smartphone—A mobile phone with advanced features such as internet access, touchscreen interface, and various applications

Social Construction of Technology—The theory that technology is shaped by social forces and constructed by societal values, norms, and institutions

Social Media—Websites and applications that enable users to create and share content or participate in social networking

Social Network—A digital platform that connects individuals or groups of people with shared interests or activities (e.g., Facebook, Instagram, Snapchat)

Streaks—A feature in social media and gaming apps where users are encouraged to maintain a consecutive daily activity streak, fostering habitual use and increasing engagement

Technological Determinism—The theory that technology shapes society and culture, influencing social structures, behaviours, and values

Technology—The application of scientific knowledge for practical purposes, especially in industry

Variable Reinforcement—A psychological principle where rewards are given on an unpredictable schedule, making the behaviour more persistent, often used in technology and social media to keep users engaged

ACKNOWLEDGMENTS

Thank you to the many inspiring teachers and coaches who have helped shape the educator I am today. You never get enough thank-yous for what you do. I also want to acknowledge my innovative colleagues (Nichelle, Scott, Tim, Kate, Susanna, and many, many others at OB) who encourage me to develop and think deeply about my practice.

A huge shout-out to my wife. Your teaching brilliance inspires me, and I could not have a better partner to climb mountains or play idea ping-pong with.

Trevor MacKenzie, this book would not be here without your belief. Thank you for saying, "Go, write it!"

Erin Casey, my editor for this book, I feel like you pulled me the last few meters to the summit, and I am happy we share a love of hiking metaphors.

And to my students, past and present, thank you for challenging me to grow and learn alongside you.

ABOUT THE AUTHOR

Lisa Green is an educator who lives and teaches in Victoria, BC. She has a desire for lifelong learning and is curious about the interdisciplinary connections that exist between organizational psychology, coaching studies, and education. She is particularly engaged with how these areas can apply to and enhance the educational practice.

CITATIONS

Baldwin, Douglas. *Teachers, Students And Pedagogy: Selected Readings and Documents in the History of Canadian Education*. Fitzhenry & Whiteside, 2008.

Barak, Moshe, et al. "Teamwork in Modern Organizations: Implications for Technology Education." *International Journal of Technology and Design Education* 9, no. 1 (1999): 85–101. https://doi:10.1023/a:1008849803984.

BC's Curriculum. "Building Student Success." Accessed October 1, 2024. https://curriculum.gov.bc.ca/curriculum/english-language-arts/12/english-studies.

BC's Curriculum. "Curriculum Overview." https://curriculum.gov.bc.ca/curriculum/overview.

Brown, J. K. "Student-Centered Instruction: Involving Students in Their Own Education." *Music Educators Journal* 94, no. 5 (2008): 30–35. https://doi.org/10.1177/00274321080940050108.

Catmull, Ed. "How Pixar Fosters Collective Creativity." *Harvard Business Review*, February 25, 2019. hbr.org/2008/09/how-pixar-fosters-collective-creativity.

Clear, James. "The 5 triggers that make new habits stick." *James Clear*, November 13, 2018. https://jamesclear.com/habit-triggers.

Cohen, Danielle. "Why Kids Need to Spend Time in Nature." *Child Mind Institute*, October 30, 2023. https://childmind.org/article/why-kids-need-to-spend-time-in-nature.

Coles, Keri. "Census 2016: Oak Bay one of most highly educated populations in world." *Victoria News*, December 1, 2017. https://www.vicnews.com/news/census-2016-oak-bay-one-of-most-highly-educated-populations-in-world.

Cross, Rob, et al. "Collaborative Overload." *Harvard Business Review*, September 11, 2020. hbr.org/2016/01/collaborative-overload.

Duhigg, Charles. "What Google Learned From Its Quest to Build the Perfect Team." *The New York Times*, February 25, 2016. https://www.nytimes.com/2016/02/28/magazine/what-google-learned-from-its-quest-to-build-the-perfect-team.html.

Edmondson, Amy C. *Teaming to Innovate*. John Wiley & Sons, 2014.

Edmondson, Amy. "The Role of Psychological Safety: Maximizing Employee Input and Commitment." *Leader to Leader* 92, 2019, *EBSCOhost*, doi:10.1002/ltl.20419.

Fu, H., Hopper, T., & Sanford, K. "New BC Curriculum and Communicating Student Learning in an Age of Assessment for Learning." *Alberta Journal of Educational Research* 63, Fall (2018).

Gacoin, Andrée. "Research: The politics of curriculum making understanding the possibilities for and limitations to a 'teacher-led' curriculum in British Columbia." *BC Teachers Federation*, August 2, 2019. https://www.bctf.ca/news-and-opportunities/news-details/2019/08/02/the-politics-of-curriculum-making-understanding-the-possibilities-for-and-limitations-to-a-teacher-led-curriculum-in-british-columbia.

Graham, M. A. "Art, Ecology and Art Education: Locating Art Education in a Critical Place-based Pedagogy." *Studies in Art Education* 48, no. 4 (2007): 375–91. https://doi.org/10.1080/00393541.2007.11650115.

Hansen, Randall S. "Benefits and Problems With Student Teams: Suggestions for Improving Team Projects." *Journal of Education for Business* 82, no. 1 (2006): 11–19.

Hari, Johann. *Stolen Focus: Why You Can't Pay Attention*. Crown Publishing, 2023.

Kanu, Y., & Glor, M. "'Currere' to the rescue? Teachers as 'amateur Intellectuals' in a knowledge society." *Journal of the Canadian Association for Curriculum Studies* 4, no. 2 (2006): 101–22.

Karl, Jessica. "The Introvert Economy Is Here to Stay." *Bloomberg.com*, January 27, 2024. https://www.bloomberg.com/opinion/articles/2024-01-27/the-introvert-economy-is-here-to-stay-lrw2xoju.

Krahenbuhl, Kevin S. "Student-Centered Education and Constructivism: Challenges, Concerns, and Clarity for Teachers." *Clearing House* 89, no. 3 (2016): 97–105. *EBSCOhost*, doi:10.1080/00098655.2016.1191311.

Le, Ha, et al. "Collaborative Learning Practices: Teacher and Student Perceived Obstacles to Effective Student Collaboration." *Cambridge Journal of Education* 48, no. 1 (2017): 103–22. doi:10.1080/0305764x.2016.1259389.

Lencioni, Patrick M. *The Five Dysfunctions of a Team*. Jossey-Bass, 2002.

Li, Ting, Lixia Cui, Shu Ma, Shuang Zhang, Jie Zheng, Jing Xiao, Qin Zhang. "An 8-Week Group Cognitive Behavioral Therapy Intervention for Mobile Dependence." *Psychology* 9, no. 8 (2018): 2031–2041. doi: 10.4236/psych.2018.98116.

Madigan, Sheri. "Assessment of Changes in Child and Adolescent Screen Time During the COVID-19 Pandemic." *JAMA Pediatrics* 176, no. 12 (2022): 1188-1198. https://jamanetwork.com/journals/jamapediatrics/fullarticle/2798256.

Meijers, Frans. "Monologue to Dialogue: Education in the 21st Century, Introduction to the Special Issue." *International Journal for Dialogical*

Science 7, no. 1 (2013): 1–10. https://ijds.lemoyne.edu/journal/7_1/pdf/IJDS.7.1.01.Meijers.pdf.

Nagata, Jason M, Catherine A. Cortez, Chloe J. Cattle, et al. "Screen Time Use Among US Adolescents During the COVID-19 Pandemic." *JAMA Pediatrics* 6, no 1 (2022): 94–96. https://jamanetwork.com/journals/jamapediatrics/fullarticle/2785686.

Pew Research Center. "Mobile Fact Sheet." April 7, 2021. https://www.pewresearch.org/internet/fact-sheet/mobile.

Richardson, Aaron. "The 15 Minute Study Strategy." *Smart Student Secrets*, February 8, 2019. https://www.smartstudentsecrets.com/the-15-minute-study-strategy.

Robinson, Phil A., director. *Field of Dreams*. Universal Pictures. 1989. 1 hr., 47 min.

Roose, Kevin. "Don't Ban ChatGPT in Schools. Teach With It." *The New York Times*, January 12, 2023. https://www.nytimes.com/2023/01/12/technology/chatgpt-schools-teachers.html.

Ross, Terrance F. "The death of textbooks." *The Atlantic*. March 6, 2015. https://www.theatlantic.com/education/archive/2015/03/the-death-of-textbooks/387055/.

Schaeffer, Katherine. "Most U. S. teens who use cellphones do it to pass time, connect with others, learn new things." *Pew Research Center*. August 23, 2019. https://www.pewresearch.org/short-reads/2019/08/23/most-u-s-teens-who-use-cellphones-do-it-to-pass-time-connect-with-others-learn-new-things/.

Schulz-Hardt, Stefan, and Felix C. Brodbeck. *Introduction to Social Psychology: A European Perspective*. Blackwell Publishing, 2011.

Schwartz, Carolyn E., and Meir Sendor. "Helping others helps oneself: response shift effects in peer support." *Social Science & Medicine* 48, no. 11 (1999): 1563–1575. https://doi.org/10.1016/S0277-9536(99)00049-0.

Seal, Rebecca. "Is your smartphone ruining your memory? A special report on the rise of 'digital amnesia.'" *The Guardian*. July 3, 2022. https://www.theguardian.com/global/2022/jul/03/is-your-smartphone-ruining-your-memory-the-rise-of-digital-amenesia.

Singh, Karan. "Unlocking the Potential of Multi-Generational Collaboration in the Workplace." *Forbes*, May 22, 2024. https://www.forbes.com/councils/forbesbusinesscouncil/2024/05/22/unlocking-the-potential-of-multi-generational-collaboration-in-the-workplace.

Skills/Compétences Canada. "Essential Skills Resources." Accessed October 1, 2024. https://www.skillscompetencescanada.com/en/program/skills-for-success.

Twenge, Jean M. "Have smartphones destroyed a generation?" *The Atlantic*. September 2017. https://www.theatlantic.com/magazine/archive/2017/09/has-the-smartphone-destroyed-a-generation/534198.

Winters, Annemie, Frans Meijers, Mariëtte Harlaar, Anneke Strik, et al. "The Narrative Quality of Career Conversations in Vocational Education." *Journal of Constructivist Psychology* 26, no. 2 (2013): 115–26. doi: 10.1080/10720537.2013.759026.

*Images created through CANVA—Artist: Zdenek Sasek

MORE FROM ELEVATE BOOKS EDU

Dive into Inquiry
Amplify Learning and Empower Student Voice
By Trevor MacKenzie

Dive into Inquiry beautifully marries the voice and choice of inquiry with the structure and support required to optimize learning. With Dive into Inquiry, you'll gain an understanding of how to best support your learners as they shift from a traditional learning model into the inquiry classroom where student agency is fostered and celebrated each and every day.

Inquiry Mindset: Elementary Edition
Nurturing the Dreams, Wonders, and Curiosities of Our Youngest Learners
By Trevor MacKenzie and Rebecca Bushby

Inquiry Mindset: Elementary Edition offers a highly accessible journey through inquiry in the younger years. Learn how to empower your students, increase engagement, and accelerate learning by harnessing the power of curiosity. With practical examples and a step-by-step guide to inquiry, Trevor MacKenzie and Rebecca Bushby make inquiry-based learning simple.

Available in English, French, Latin American Spanish, and European Spanish

Inquiry Mindset: Assessment Edition
Scaffolding a Partnership for Equity and Agency in Learning
By Trevor MacKenzie

Trevor MacKenzie takes another deep dive into inquiry as he examines the role of assessment in education through the lens of co-designing and co-constructing with students. In *Inquiry Mindset: Assessment Edition*, he outlines the beliefs, values, and frameworks that allow teachers to scaffold assessments infused with student voice, understanding, and autonomy.

Inquiry Mindset: Questions Edition
Cultivating Curiosity and Creating Question Competence
By Trevor MacKenzie

The Question Routines and teacher insights in *Inquiry Mindset: Questions Edition* provide a framework that you and your students can use to craft, organize, and justify questions. Effective across grade levels and subject areas, the strategies MacKenzie provides will empower you to bring fresh excitement and engagement to the learning experience.

Getting Personal with Inquiry Learning
Guiding Learners' Explorations of Personal Passions, Interests and Questions
By Kath Murdoch

In *Getting Personal with Inquiry Learning*, world-renowned inquiry expert, Kath Murdoch, draws on decades of experience to offer a thorough, practical guide to supporting young learners' investigations into their passions, interests, and questions. Following on from the best-selling Power of Inquiry, this book invites teachers to take their thinking about inquiry to the next level and to truly honor both their own and their students' agency.

From Agency to Zest
A Journey through the Landscape of Inquiry
By Kath Murdoch

The delightfully thought-provoking words in this exploration of inquiry-based learning embody the essence of inquiry. Designed to be used to initiate reflection and to provoke professional dialogue amongst educators, *From Agency to Zest* offers insight into inquiry as an approach to teaching and learning. In addition to the explanations provided throughout, Murdoch offers practical advice on how to support and deepen professional learning experiences within and across schools.

CITATIONS | 195

Leading with a Lens of Inquiry
Cultivating Conditions for Curiosity and Empowering Agency
By Jessica Vance

Typical models of training and professional development focus on telling. It's a model that far too often trickles down to classrooms where the traditional way of "doing school" limits the way educators teach and students learn. Fortunately, there is a better way to learn: through wonder, agency, and inquiry. From *Leading with a Lens of Inquiry* administrators, educational instructors, and peer leaders learn how to cultivate learning spaces that ignite curiosity and inspire critical thinking in adult and student learners alike.

Taking the Complexities Out of Concepts
By by Tania Lattanzio and Andrea Muller

This practical resource designed by Innovative Global Education (IGE) helps educators shift from a content-based curriculum to a conceptual curriculum. Teaching through concepts provides context that leads to the transferability of knowledge. Using the strategies and ideas in *Taking the Complexities Out of Concepts,* students will develop connections to and a deep understanding of the material.

The AI Infused Classroom
Inspiring Ideas to Shift Teaching and Maximize Meaningful Learning in the World of AI
By Holly Clark

With the right mindset, the right questions, and the right strategies, you can use AI to create and broaden meaningful learning experiences for every student. In *The AI Infused Classroom*, Holly Clark points out that students need well-trained educators now more than ever, to ensure they are prepared for the world of AI. This book equips you to navigate the latest iteration of edtech.

The Google Infused Classroom
A Guidebook to Making Thinking Visible and Amplifying Student Voice
By Holly Clark and Tanya Avrith

This beautifully designed book offers guidance on using technology to design instruction that allows students to show their thinking, demonstrate their learning, and share their work (and voices!) with authentic audiences. *The Google Infused Classroom* will equip you to empower your students to use technology in meaningful ways that prepare them for the future.

The Microsoft Infused Classroom
A Guidebook to Making Thinking Visible and Amplifying Student Voice
By Holly Clark and Tanya Avrith

Packed with ideas you can use in your classroom tomorrow, *The Microsoft Infused Classroom*, equips you to use powerful tools that put learning first. Edtech experts led by Holly Clark and Tanya Avrith show you how to use technology to increase engagement in your classroom and provide authentic opportunities for students to share their work and their voice.

The Chromebook Infused Classroom
Using Blended Learning to Create Engaging, Student-Centered Classrooms
By Holly Clark

Edtech expert and trainer Holly Clark serves as your guide to using Chromebooks effectively in the classroom. As with other books in the *Infused Classroom* series, *The Chromebook Infused Classroom* relies on proven pedagogical practices to create engaging and meaningful learning experiences for today's students. With its wealth of tools, ideas, and step-by-step instructions, this book equips you to empower your students for learning—and for life.

The InterACTIVE Class
Using Technology to Make Learning more Relevant and Engaging in the Elementary Classroom
By Joe and Kristin Merrill

In this practical and idea-packed book, coauthors, classroom teachers, and edtech experts Joe and Kristin Merrill share their personal framework for creating an interACTIVE classroom. You'll find new ways to inspire young learners to grow and to develop grit as they stretch their thinking and abilities.

Flipgrid in the InterACTIVE Class
Encouraging Inclusion and Student Voice in the Elementary
By Joe and Kristin Merrill

Classroom teachers Joe and Kristin Merrill have seen firsthand how the practical ideas shared in *Flipgrid in the InterACTIVE Class* impact learning. By equipping teachers to design more opportunities for students to share their voices and create more equitable learning experiences, Flipgrid opens the door for interaction and discussion in the elementary classroom.

Sketchnotes for Educators
100 Inspiring Illustrations for Lifelong Learners
By Sylvia Duckworth

Sylvia Duckworth is a Canadian teacher whose sketchnotes have taken social media by storm. Her drawings provide clarity and provoke dialogue on many topics related to education. This book contains 100 of her most popular sketchnotes with links to the original downloads that can be used in class or shared with colleagues. Interspersed throughout the book are Sylvia's reflections on each drawing and what motivated her to create them, in addition to commentary from other educators who inspired the sketchnotes.

How to Sketchnote
Visual Note-taking Made Easy
By Sylvia Duckworth

Educator and internationally known sketchnoter Sylvia Duckworth makes ideas memorable and shareable with her simple yet powerful drawings. In *How to Sketchnote*, she explains how you can use sketchnoting in the classroom and that you don't have to be an artist to discover the benefits of doodling!

40 Ways to Inject Creativity into Your Classroom with A
By Ben Forta and Monica Burns

Experienced educators Ben Forta and Monica Burns offer step-by-step guidance on how to incorporate this powerful tool into your classroom in ways that are meaningful and relevant. They present 40 fun and practical lesson plans suitable for a variety of ages and subjects as well as 15 graphic organizers to get you started. With the tips, suggestions, and encouragement in this book, you'll find everything you need to inject creativity into your classroom using Adobe Spark.

The HyperDoc Handbook
Digital Lesson Design Using Google Apps
By Lisa Highfill, Kelly Hilton, and Sarah Landis

The HyperDoc Handbook is a practical reference guide for all K–12 educators who want to transform their teaching into blended-learning environments. *The HyperDoc Handbook* is a bestselling book that strikes the perfect balance between pedagogy and how-to tips while also providing ready-to-use lesson plans to get you started with HyperDocs right away.

www.ingramcontent.com/pod-product-compliance
Lightning Source LLC
Chambersburg PA
CBHW070622030426
42337CB00020B/3885